BEST WISHES

BOOK 4

Like a Boss

ALSO BY SARAH MLYNOWSKI

The *Whatever After* series

The *Upside-Down Magic* series,
cowritten with Emily Jenkins and Lauren Myracle

Best Wishes #1

Best Wishes #2: The Sister Switch,
cowritten with Debbie Rigaud

Best Wishes #3: Time After Time,
cowritten with Christina Soontornvat

Fairest of All: The Graphic Novel (Whatever After Graphic Novel #1), illustrated by Anu Chouhan

A Dragon for Hanukkah, illustrated by Ariel Landy

ALSO BY HENA KHAN

We Are Big Time, illustrated by Safiya Zerrougui

Drawing Deena

More to the Story

Amina's Voice

Amina's Song

The *Zara's Rules* series

The *Zayd Saleem* series

The *Super You!* series

Best Wishes

Book 4

Like a Boss

SARAH MLYNOWSKI AND
HENA KHAN

Illustrations by Jen Bricking

Scholastic Press
New York

Library of Congress Cataloging-in-Publication Data available

ISBN 978-93-5954-425-0

First edition, 2024

This reprint edition November 2024

Book design by Abby Dening and Elizabeth B. Parisi

Printed in India at Shivam Offset Press, New Delhi

To our readers, the future leaders of the world.

We can't wait.

—S.M. & H.K.

*

* 1 *

Hold the Glitter

Dear Emma,

This isn't junk mail!

I know that: 1) You don't know who I am, and 2) if you're like my grandmother, who I call Dadi, you probably think this is some kind of scam.

But I promise . . . it's not a scam. Or junk mail.

My name is Maya Amir, and I live in Washington, DC. And before I say more, don't put on the bracelet yet. Please! Read to the end of this letter first. You will thank me later.

You're probably even more confused now, huh?

I think the best way to explain is to just tell you everything that happened to me. And then you'll understand. But seriously, take that bracelet off if you're already wearing it! I mean it!

It all started on Friday, which is my favorite day of the week. Every Friday, my family does movie night at home and we order takeout from our favorite Thai place.

Not that my older sister and brother EVER let me pick the movie—I'm the youngest, and I don't get a lot of say—but it's still super fun.

Most importantly, *this* Friday was the first day of club meetings after school. Which meant I would finally, FINALLY get to be in the environmental club with my best friend, Hazel Garcia.

It was 2:45 p.m., and I could barely pay attention in class. I had wanted to be in the environmental club for *years*, but it was only for fifth graders. Now that I was in the fifth grade, this was my chance to share some of my big ideas for helping the planet.

My teacher, Ms. Sokolov, was reviewing a social studies worksheet about constitutional power and the branches of government. I half listened, waiting for the final bell to ring.

"Laws are voted on by Congress in the Capitol Building, right here in our very own backyard," Ms. Sokolov said.

The teachers at my school, Summit Elementary, love to

brag about the fact that we're close to all the famous national monuments here in DC. Although we're not *that* close. You can catch a glimpse of the dome of the Capitol out the window, but only if you really crane your neck.

The bell rang and I jumped out of my seat.

"Your short story assignment is due on Monday!" Ms. Sokolov called while we all rushed to pack up our things. "And as you leave, you can each choose one of the cupcakes Leo's mom dropped off. Happy birthday, Leo!"

Leo Rosenblatt turned bright red. He's quiet and doesn't like being the center of attention.

But, yay, cupcakes!

Hazel and I stepped up to the teacher's desk and checked out the options.

Chocolate-chocolate. Vanilla-chocolate. Red velvet. Vanilla with purple icing. Which one did I want? My stomach grumbled. So many choices . . .

I'm not great at choosing. I'm always worried I'm going to pick the wrong thing.

Hazel grabbed a red velvet cupcake and licked off a chunk of the icing. "Yum. My favorite. Take one, Maya! There's only one red velvet left."

Um . . . um . . . but did I really want red velvet?

Another girl in our class, Maddie Northrup, stepped up and picked the last red velvet cupcake from the box while I was still deciding.

Darn it.

Hmm. The chocolate-chocolate one looked good, but what if it was too chocolatey? The vanilla one looked good, too, but what if its purple icing stained my lips?

I picked the vanilla one with chocolate icing, then immediately regretted it. What a boring choice. But it was too late to change my mind.

"Ready?" Hazel asked, still licking her icing. She was wearing a T-shirt, jeans, and sneakers, which looked a whole lot like my outfit, except her T-shirt said *Supergirl* on it, and mine said *Shenandoah National Park*. We've always dressed a lot alike, although we don't look anything alike. I've got brown skin, dark brown eyes, and dark, thick, wavy hair that comes to my shoulders. Hazel has long, light brown hair and light brown eyes. Plus, I'm at least three inches taller than my bestie and I've got purple-framed glasses. Purple is my favorite color.

I really should have taken the cupcake with the purple icing. Purple lips would have been cool.

"Ready," I repeated as I followed Hazel out the door.

Hazel was also excited about the club. Maybe not as excited as I was, but she is really into science. Last year, we got an honorable mention in the science fair for our very cool yet very disgusting project on mold. It was my idea—I have a lot of ideas, actually—and Hazel liked that one the best.

Today, I had a ton of ideas for the environmental club. I'd written them all down in my new biodegradable notebook that I was bringing to the meeting. I couldn't wait!

Hazel and I walked into Ms. Maxwell's science room. Ms. Maxwell is the club's sponsor. There were eight other kids there.

"Hi, everyone, welcome to the environmental club!" Ms. Maxwell said in her cheery way. She had her curly hair pulled into a messy bun on top of her head, and she twirled a pencil between her fingers as she talked. "I know you're all here because you care about the future of our planet, and the ways we can ensure it's a nice place to live for a long time."

Everyone murmured their agreement. Hazel and I took our seats and I quietly nibbled on my cupcake, feeling hopeful. This was going to be great.

"First off, we need to elect a club president," Ms. Maxwell continued. "Who would like to nominate themselves for the role?"

Oh, wow. President? I didn't realize there were presidents of clubs! Being the president would mean I'd definitely get to share all my ideas with the group.

I could be president.

Could I?

Maybe?

Hazel turned to me.

"You should do it, Maya!" she whispered.

"Me?" I mumbled with my mouth full. Nervous excitement

sent a shiver through me. I'd never been in charge of anything before. "What about you?" I asked Hazel.

"I'd be great, too. One of us should definitely be president!" Hazel said. "Who knows more about the environment than we do?"

Hazel had a point.

Not to brag, but I do know a lot about the environment, mostly because Dadi has taught me so much. My grandmother used to head an environmental protection organization in Pakistan before she moved in with us here in DC. And now Dadi and I do cool projects together, like our indoor hydroponic garden. We started off small, but slowly our garden took over half the storage room. You should see the stuff Dadi and I grow together—everything from cilantro to hot peppers.

And then I got Hazel interested in the environment, too, by showing her how it all connected to science, which Hazel loves.

"Anyone?" Ms. Maxwell asked, looking around the room.

My heart pounded. *Should I raise my hand?*

I imagined going home and telling my family that I was

president of the environmental club. They'd be so surprised! And Dadi would burst with pride.

Although . . . Hazel was better at making decisions than I was. In fact, she usually made decisions for me.

Should I let Hazel do it instead? I wondered.

But I had all these new ideas, written in my notebook!

But what if nobody liked my ideas?

I didn't know what to do.

Hazel looked at me with her eyebrows raised, and I shrugged, still debating whether or not to nominate myself.

Ms. Maxwell clicked her pen. "Okay, well, if there isn't anyone interested, I will just—"

"I'll do it," Hazel said. "I'll be president."

She will?

"Great!" Ms. Maxwell said. "Anyone else want to put in their name? We could vote."

Even though I kind of wanted to raise my hand, I was frozen. How could I run against Hazel?

I couldn't. That had to be against the best friend rules.

Right?

I glanced at Hazel, who looked nervous and bit her lip while we waited to see if anyone else nominated themselves.

The way she squeezed my arm in excitement made it clear to me: I couldn't run against her.

"If there are no other candidates, then you are our president, Hazel Garcia. Congratulations!" Ms. Maxwell handed Hazel a folder. "I'll be at my desk grading papers if you need me, but you should all get started and discuss your plans for the club."

Hazel grinned at me, and then stood up and faced the group, blushing a little.

I swallowed my disappointment. *It's fine*, I thought. *I can still contribute as a regular member, if not the leader. And anyway, I'm sure Hazel will listen to all my ideas, so I'll still make a difference.*

"Hi, everyone," Hazel said. "I think the first thing we need to do is make this club bigger and better than ever before. We could use more members, right?"

I was sort of surprised that was Hazel's first priority, but I supposed bringing in more members couldn't hurt. Everyone nodded.

"So . . ." Hazel paused for dramatic effect. "Let's advertise all over the school."

"Why don't we put up lots of posters in the hallway?" a

girl named Cassandra suggested. "And make flyers to hand out to students."

"Good thinking!" Hazel said, beaming.

What? I stared at Hazel as hard as I could, but she was focused on Cassandra.

"We can decorate the posters and flyers with paint and glitter," Cassandra continued, and Hazel nodded.

"Isn't using all that paper, you know, bad for the environ—" I started to say.

"And we could have a big party to kick off the year!" Hazel interrupted me. "Maybe we could get Leo to join the club, so his mom could donate some more of those cupcakes, because they're the best I've ever tried."

"What about trying something like composting, or—" I said, a little louder.

But nobody, including Hazel, was listening to me. They were all pumped about the party idea and started discussing their favorite cupcake flavors and what kind of glitter to use for the posters. It was like I wasn't even there anymore, and my stomach started churning. This was definitely *not* the club I'd been waiting to join for the past two years.

I mean, I love parties and cupcakes—who doesn't? But not for the environmental club! We were supposed to do things like stop waste, and plant trees, and make a difference. And besides, glitter is a microplastic and totally a pollutant!

"We'll talk about it more next week," Hazel said. "Also, Fridays are meant for relaxing, so if it's okay with Ms. Maxwell, let's have our regular meetings on Mondays. Ms. Maxwell?"

"Hmm?" Ms. Maxwell asked, looking up from her papers.

"Can we move this meeting to Mondays?"

"Sure," Ms. Maxwell replied.

That was the only suggestion from Hazel that made sense to me. But I didn't know if I wanted to come back on Monday. I didn't know if I still wanted to be *part* of this club. And I kind of felt like all of a sudden I didn't know Hazel anymore.

"That was awesome, wasn't it?" Hazel asked me as we left the room together. She looked so pleased that I didn't know what to say to her.

"It was"—horrible! upsetting!—"*interesting,*" I said with a weak smile. And then I thought to myself, *I guess things can't get worse.*

I was wrong.

Fifteen minutes after Hazel got picked up, I was still sitting on the bench outside school, waiting for my older sister,

Natasha. She's in high school, and she picks me up if I don't take the school bus home. But she was so late today. Ugh!

I finally went to the main office and called her.

Natasha has her own phone. I do not.

"Maya?" Natasha answered. "Where are you?"

"I had my club meeting after school. Aren't you supposed to get me?"

Silence.

"Oh my gosh, Maya. I forgot! Dadi needed me to get some stuff from the desi store and . . . I'll be there as fast as I can!"

When Natasha finally pulled up in our green minivan, I was literally the last person other than the custodian still at school. And I was furious.

"I can't believe you forgot me," I sulked on the ride home.

"I'm sorry!" my sister said again. "You should have reminded me this morning."

"I've been talking about my club meeting for weeks," I grumbled.

"I don't remember . . . What club is it?"

"Never mind," I said as I tried to shake off my frustration. I didn't want to talk about the club, or how the meeting had been a disaster, anyway.

At least I had movie night to look forward to. I just hoped my brother, Omar, wouldn't pull the same prank on me that he had last week: He switched the candies in the boxes, so when I opened my favorite, sour gummies, I got stale raisins instead.

Yes. Stale raisins.

Omar's obsessed with this YouTube show where a group of friends play practical jokes on each other and other people. It's pretty funny, except that it inspires Omar to prank our whole family. The other day, he placed black steel wool in the shape of a spider on our dad's pillow, because Baba gets freaked out by anything that crawls. And it worked! Pranks are really big with all the seventh-grade boys this year, apparently.

When Natasha and I got home, we found Dadi in the kitchen. She was wearing a stained Eiffel Tower apron over her flowing shalwar kameez, stirring a giant pot of chicken korma on the stove, and shouting orders at my parents and Omar, who were busy cleaning in the living room.

My grandmother is barely five feet tall, if you count the white-hair-streaked bun on top of her head, but when she speaks, people listen. And even though she usually mixes Urdu into her English, my siblings and I understand her perfectly. She's been living with us for as long as I can remember.

"What's going on?" I asked Dadi.

"Your auntie and Sabrina will be here in two hours," Dadi said. "There's so much to do!"

I frowned. This was the first I was hearing about this visit. My mom's cousin and her daughter live in Pittsburgh. "Why are they coming?" I asked.

"Sabrina is touring colleges in the area," Natasha explained.

"They'll be staying in your room, Maya," Dadi told me. "So you'll be moving into my room with me."

"They will? I will?" I asked. "No one told me!"

"Of course we did," Natasha said, shaking her head. "Didn't we?"

"No!"

I frowned. My family never tells me anything. It's like they think nothing affects me because I'm the youngest, so there's no need to include me in family business or decisions.

It's super annoying.

"I already got your pajamas for you, but you should take out your clothes for tomorrow from your room," Dadi told me as my parents walked into the kitchen. Mama was holding a duster, and Baba held the empty recycling bin.

"Why do Auntie and Sabrina have to stay in MY room?" I complained to my parents, even though I knew the answer.

"You're the youngest, and it's easiest for you to move," Mama replied, exactly as I expected.

"What about movie night? Can we still do it?" I asked, somehow still feeling hopeful.

"Not tonight, kiddo," Baba said, looking a bit disappointed himself.

Dadi shook her head. "It's okay, we will do it next time! Now go, go and do what I asked. They'll be here soon!"

I let out a sigh and went into my—for now—room to pick out clothes. Dadi had already vacuumed and made my bed. There was even a vase of fresh-cut flowers on my nightstand for our guests. How nice for them.

"And those are just the schools I'm looking at on the East Coast," Sabrina said, taking another bite of daal.

The eight of us were sitting around the dining room table, and I kept fidgeting. Sure, I was happy to see my cousin, but she was mostly talking to Natasha, since they're almost the same age.

Instead of watching a movie and eating my favorite takeout—shrimp pad thai—I had to have boring chicken korma, daal, and aloo gobi (Auntie's favorite foods), and listen to even more boring college talk.

"Will you have any time for sightseeing?" my mom asked Auntie, who nodded. "Natasha, where do you think we should take them?"

"It depends." Natasha started to rattle off suggestions a mile a minute, and my mind drifted back to the environmental club meeting. I was still upset with Hazel for stealing the presidency. Although maybe it was my fault for freezing up. But either way—her ideas were terrible.

"Earth to Maya," Omar said, waving his fork in front of my face.

"What?" I said, snapping out of my thoughts.

"Auntie asked you what your favorite subject is," Baba said.

"Um, I think it's science," I said. "Or history. I really like math, too, but I'm better at science. Or maybe English. I'm not sure."

Auntie smiled. "Well, it's good to have lots of interests," she said while my face warmed from embarrassment. Why couldn't I decide on something so simple?

"Omar and Natasha," Dadi said, "please clear the plates while I bring out dessert."

"What about Maya?" Omar asked. "Why doesn't she ever have to do anything?"

"I'm still eating," I pointed out.

"You're eating slow on purpose," Omar said.

"She never puts the dishes in the dishwasher properly anyway," Natasha said.

"Leave her alone," Dadi said, setting her hand protectively on my shoulder. Sometimes it was good to be the baby of the family. Dadi always looked out for me.

I glared at Omar and swirled the food around on my plate. Everything was all mixed up into a mush, just like my thoughts and feelings. How had this day turned out to be such a disappointing mess?

Dessert was followed by chai for the grown-ups, and more talking. Everyone asked Natasha about her future plans, how she rated all the kabob restaurants in town, and her opinion on some Indian movie. Natasha acts like she knows everything, and somehow everyone in my family believes it.

But the night still wasn't over. I had to sleep on the old air mattress in Dadi's room.

I love Dadi.

I do not love the old air mattress.

Especially when, in the middle of the night, I was tossing and turning and . . . *phhhhhhhhhhhhfffft*! The air mattress gave up on its job and completely deflated.

Dadi doesn't have a carpet in her room, so I was basically sleeping on a wooden floor. Ouch.

And then I heard . . .

CHHHHHHHHHHNNNOOOOOOOOORT.

Whiiiiiiiistle.

CHHHHHHHHHHNNNOOOOOOOOORT.

Whiiiiiiiistle.

I forgot that my grandmother snores. Loudly.

Argh.

As I tossed and turned, and turned and tossed, I stared at the ceiling and muttered to myself, "Worst day ever."

I could see the lights in the hallway flicker through the crack under the door. A burst of cold air passed right through my blanket. Great. Now it was cold in here, too. I flipped back onto my stomach, pulled my pillow over my head, and tried again to fall asleep.

✶ 2 ✶

The Box Arrives

The next day, my mom, Natasha, Auntie, and Sabrina went to take a tour of Georgetown University, so the rest of us were left to do our own thing. I was feeling pretty grumpy after my terrible night of sleep. Normally, I would text Hazel to complain, but since I was *also* grumpy about the club situation, I decided to do my homework instead. I had to write a two-page short story and I wasn't sure what to write about. A girl whose family came to visit so she had to sleep on her grandmother's floor?

I sat down at the kitchen table and started writing.

Then I worried that the beginning wasn't good, so I began again.

And then again.

Around three o'clock, after starting nine different drafts, I was finally finishing up when Omar casually walked over and said, "Hey, you got a package."

"From who?" I asked. I hardly ever get packages.

I studied Omar suspiciously. Was this one of his pranks?

"I don't know. It's not from me," he snorted.

"Where is it?" I demanded.

Omar pointed to the table in the entrance hall. I hurried over and saw a shiny red box sitting on it. There was a pink ribbon around the box, and my name and address were clearly written in big letters across the top.

Maya Amir
1267 Albemarle Street NW
Washington, DC 20016

It didn't have a return address, though. Weird.

I glanced at Omar again. Was there going to be a giant bug or some dog poop inside?

"So, what's in it?" Omar asked, sounding curious. "Is it candy? It looks like candy. Are you going to share? You better share!"

Maybe the box wasn't from him?

"I don't know yet!" I looked around for a private place, away from Omar, to open up the package. Baba was reading in the living room, and Dadi was in her room taking a nap. Since my room wasn't mine anymore—Auntie's and Sabrina's things were there, and they could come back at any moment—I decided the laundry room would have to work.

Once I was safely alone, I rested the box on the dryer.

Who could this package be from? I had no idea. My birthday is in August. And the people who normally sent me gifts by mail—like my auntie and Sabrina—were here. Maybe my mom or dad had ordered me something as a surprise?

I removed the wrapping carefully. Inside was a velvet pouch, a white notebook, and an old-fashioned piece of paper with a poem written on it.

Because you're blue,
This bracelet is now for you.
Speak one wish to make it true.
(There are some things it cannot do.)
Keep the box to mail the magic off
When you are through.
Take care and beware.
Hugs and kisses,
And best wishes.

Bracelet? Wishes? Blue?

I definitely was feeling blue. After the club meeting and then being kicked out of my room . . . and my neck still hurt from the night on the floor. But no one else knew I was blue. It wasn't like I was running around screaming the news.

It wasn't like my family had asked me how *my* day was yesterday.

And what bracelet?

Was it in the pouch?

I spilled the contents of the pouch into my hand. Yup, definitely a bracelet. It was made of different-sized green and gold beads.

Pretty. Who was it from? Why was there a weird old-timey poem instead of a card?

There was no clasp on the bracelet, but it slipped right over my hand and onto my wrist.

It fit perfectly. And it looked good.

What was the deal with the notebook?

I opened it to the front page.

Hi Maya,

I'm Lucy. You don't know me—yet. But I'm here to tell you about the most amazing thing that has ever happened to me.

And to you.

I got this mysterious box in the mail, just like you did. I was dazzled by the bracelet inside, just like you probably are right now. And just like you, I got a letter that explained exactly what the bracelet was and how to use it.

I vowed not to make any of the mistakes that other people made with this magical (yes, that's right—*magical*) bracelet.

Things didn't exactly go according to plan.

I'm going to try my very best to explain what happened to me with this bracelet. I feel like I owe you that much. And the rest? That's up to you.

I put the notebook down on the dryer.

The rest was up to me.

What rest?

I picked up the poem and reread it.

Speak one wish to make it true.

This poem and this notebook were saying that the bracelet on my wrist . . . had magical powers?

Hah.

No. No way.

It couldn't be real. It just couldn't. There was no such thing as a magic bracelet. Was there? No.

Totally impossible.

But how did this Lucy person know my address? Why did she send it to *me*?

Maybe it wasn't really from Lucy. Maybe it *was* from Omar. Was he just getting better at acting?

Was he waiting to see my reaction? To see if I believed that some girl had sent me a magic bracelet? It had to be him.

I picked up the notebook again.

Hi Maya . . .

Hmm. Omar had terrible handwriting and typed everything he could. I flipped through the pages. Whoever wrote this had nice handwriting. It would have taken Omar hours and hours and hours to pull this off. And Omar spent five to ten minutes on his pranks, max, not hours and hours.

And then there was the bracelet. It was really pretty. And it looked kind of expensive. Would Omar have spent actual money on a prank? His own money? It wasn't like he had bought the steel wool to scare our dad—he had just found it under the kitchen sink.

But this . . . I touched the shiny beads. This was fancy.

I picked up the notebook again. Where was I? Oh, right. Lucy's story.

Everything started Friday, yesterday (though by the end of my story, simple words like "yesterday" are going to have a whole other meaning).

I kept reading. And reading. I heard people talking and stomping all around the house. I paused but didn't hear my name being called. Nobody was looking for me, or noticed I was missing. I guess sometimes it's helpful when people forget to tell me things—or forget about me completely.

So, I climbed on top of the dryer and kept reading.

When I got to the end, I put the notebook down.

Wow.

Lucy's story was hilarious. And bonkers. And sounded completely impossible. She claimed to have been stuck in a time loop!

And the magic hadn't just happened to her. There were two other girls, Becca Singer in New York City and Addie

Asante in Columbus, Ohio, who both had received the same magic bracelet before it got to Lucy. And there was a creepy blond woman named Eloise who was trying to steal the bracelet from whoever had it!

In the back of the notebook, Lucy included her email address along with Becca's and Addie's.

Three other people had already gotten this bracelet.

I was the fourth?

I slid off the dryer and sank to the floor.

Hmm. For some reason this Lucy person was clearly trying to get me to believe a fake story.

Although . . .

I didn't know . . .

It kind of *felt* like it was true. The details were so specific. And no one was asking me for anything, like money or personal information. So, why would Lucy be trying to trick me?

Was I being gullible?

Should I email Lucy?

Maybe. Yes. No.

If only I could find out if she was a real person. How could I do that?

Of course! The internet! I could look her up. Where was

my iPhone? Probably in my room. I hadn't looked at it since yesterday. It wasn't a real iPhone—it didn't have a phone number anymore—but when my mom had gotten her new phone, I was allowed to keep her old one to use just with Wi-Fi for texting and listening to audiobooks.

I opened the laundry room door and ran to my room. The door was closed.

I knocked. Yup. This was what it had come to—I had to knock on my own door.

"Come in!" Auntie called.

Then I had to make a good five minutes of chitchat so I wouldn't be rude, until I could finally take the phone off my desk. I ran with it back to the laundry room.

I googled *Lucy Usathorn.*

There were no hits. Hmm. But there were a bunch for a *Daniel Usathorn.* Who worked at a museum in Texas . . .

Yup. That was Lucy's dad! The one she said proposed to her school librarian! I scrolled through the images of him . . . and finally found one of him with a girl, but she looked younger than ten. Seven, maybe. I clicked on it. The caption said, *Dr. Usathorn, with his daughter, Lucy.* It was dated three years ago. Which made her ten now.

Lucy was a real person.

Did that mean her story was real?

Did that mean magic was real?

I debated googling Becca and Addie, to see what I could learn about them.

But then, before I could chicken out, I typed Lucy's email address into iMessage.

Me: Hi. I got your package.

Immediately, I saw the three dots that meant someone was writing back. My heart jumped. Then the response came.

Lucy: MAYA!!!

Lucy: Yay! Adding the others!

Becca added.

Addie added.

Lucy: Maya got the bracelet!

Becca: Hurrah! Hi, Maya! Nice to meet you! Are you totally freaked out? You must be totally freaked out.

Addie: Hiiiiiiiii!

Becca: We're real people, we promise.

Lucy: And we're super nice.

Addie: I've been waiting to hear something ever since Lucy sent the box.

Becca: Me too! That didn't take too long though.

Lucy: I just sent it today!

Addie: Maya? You still there?

I hesitated, my fingers hovering over the keyboard. Then I finally responded:

Me: Still here.

Becca: Are you freaked out by all of this?

Me: I'm just not sure what all of this . . . is.

Suddenly, my FaceTime rang. It was Lucy and the others. Should I answer?

Yes, I should.

"Hi, Maya," Lucy said. I knew it was her from the photo I'd seen online. She looked older now, with longer straight dark hair and bangs.

"I'm Becca," said the girl with super-curly blond hair. She was chewing the end of a pencil.

"Hello, Maya," said Addie. She had her dark hair in a high bun on top of her head, and a big smile. "I'm Addie."

"Hey," I said. "I'm Maya. And I'm hiding in my laundry room."

They all laughed.

"So . . ." I said. "Is this . . . for real?"

All three nodded.

"We know it sounds unbelievable," Addie said. "Really we do."

"I wish we could prove it to you . . . or show you our bracelets," Lucy said. "But we don't have them anymore—it's all the same bracelet. It just changes color."

"I wish I had taken a picture of myself wearing it," Addie said. "Or me as my sister Sophie wearing it. See, my sisters and I switched bodies—"

"Lucy wrote about it in the book," I said.

"I lived the same day over and over again," Lucy said. "So if I had taken pictures on any of my repeating Fridays, they would have disappeared the next day."

"Oh, oh, oh!" Becca said. "I did take a picture! One sec."

For a second her face was paused and we could only hear her voice.

"This was when I started a Friendstagram account," she

continued. “I took the account down but I still have the pictures. Sending to the group! Look!”

I clicked on the picture and saw that yes, Becca was indeed wearing a beaded bracelet that looked a lot like mine. It was *real*. She was wearing a *real* bracelet.

The only difference was that unlike mine, hers was turquoise.

“Mine is light green!” I said, showing my wrist to the girls.

“Ooooh,” said Becca. “Pretty.”

“The different colors are part of the magic,” Addie explained. “So do you believe us now?”

“I don’t know,” I said, playing with the beads. “I don’t NOT believe you.” They seemed nice enough. Sweet. Excited. Not like psychopaths?

“Okay, so you’re open to the possibility,” Addie said, nodding. “Excellent. That’s important for making a good wish.”

“There is no reason for us to lie,” Lucy said. “You might as well try making a wish. If nothing happens, nothing happens.”

“Something *will* happen,” Becca said knowingly. “Unless you’ve already made your wish. You haven’t yet, have you?”

I shook my head.

"What are you going to wish for?" asked Addie.

"I don't know," I said. "How does it work, exactly?"

"As soon as you make a wish, you feel the bracelet warm up and whatever you asked for becomes true . . . pretty much right away," Becca explained.

"Mine took until the next morning!" Lucy offered.

"Right. But still, you have to be careful and say something you really want," Addie said. "You're lucky you have us here to help you, Maya. I made my wish by complete accident. I was mad at my sister, and I wished to switch places with her and . . . POOF. The next thing I knew, I *was* her."

"I wished, on purpose, that everyone would want to be my friend," Becca said. "And then everyone wanted to be my friend. And I mean *everyone*. My principal. My mom. It got weird."

"I wished on purpose, too," Lucy said. "I wanted a do-over day. I just didn't expect to keep living the same day over and over and over again."

"So, decide carefully," Becca warned.

"And wish for something great," Addie said.

I gulped. No pressure.

"Like what?" I asked.

"Maybe to win the lottery?" Becca said.

That *had* already crossed my mind.

"But the wish doesn't last forever," Lucy said. "Eventually, it stops. So then you'd lose all the money."

"Well, we don't know that for sure," Addie said. "We took our bracelets off. But no one said we had to. Maybe you could keep the bracelet on and be rich forever."

"Maybe," Lucy said, biting her lip.

"What about world peace?" I asked.

"That would be a very nice wish," Addie said, nodding.

"Or no more pollution," I said, thinking about the environmental club.

"That too!" Becca said.

"We don't know what is and isn't possible, though," Lucy said. "There are some things the bracelet cannot do, right? That's what the poem says."

"Don't rush," Becca told me. "Take your time. Come up with something really amazing. Something you've always dreamt about. And then make your wish."

"Maya!" I heard my mom calling from the other side of the door. "Has anyone seen Maya?"

"I have to go," I said quickly. "But I'll . . ."

"Speak to us soon?" asked Becca.

"Wish for something great?" asked Lucy.

"Be careful?" asked Addie.

"All three," I said, before disconnecting the call.

I shook my head—in amazement, in disbelief—as I stood up.

Had that really happened?

I looked at my bracelet.

Was it actually magic?

I had no idea. But there was a way to find out. All I had to do was pick something to wish for.

* 3 *

So Many Wishes

The next morning, as we all piled into the minivan, I was still trying to decide on my wish.

"Everyone ready?" Mama called out.

Mama and Baba sat in the front. Dadi, Sabrina, and Auntie were in the middle, and, of course, I was squished in between Natasha and Omar in the backy-back.

We turned onto Rock Creek Parkway and headed to the National Mall.

I was only half paying attention as Baba pointed out the various landmarks we drove past. The Kennedy Center. The Lincoln Memorial. The Washington Monument. I gently touched the green beads with my fingertip.

I was wearing the bracelet under the sleeve of my sweatshirt so no one would notice it. Natasha and Omar would definitely tell me there was no such thing as a wish-granting bracelet.

And I didn't want to hear that. I wanted to choose a wish.

Only what?

Did I want to be famous?

Did I want to travel through time?

Did I want a million more wishes?

Omar accidentally elbowed me.

Did I want a bigger car?

We took some turns and stopped at a red light that gave us a clear view of the White House.

"It looks so much bigger in photos," Auntie said, sounding a little bit disappointed. "Can we go inside?"

"You need tickets to get inside," Mama said. "So not today, but we can try to get some for you and Sabrina next week."

Next week? How long are they staying? Should I wish for a guest house?

I've lived in DC my whole life and I've *never* been inside

the White House. I've seen most of the monuments and a bunch of the museums. But whenever someone visits, we always take them to two places: the National Gallery of Art and the Air and Space Museum. That's because 1) they're the best museums in the world, 2) you don't need advance tickets, and 3) they're free.

Our first stop, as expected, was the National Gallery of Art.

"Where should we start?" Baba asked the family as we stood at the entrance, surrounded by giant marble columns. "East building, west building, or sculpture garden?"

"East building!" Omar shouted before I could decide on what to vote for.

"East building it is," Baba said, and Omar gloated as we headed into the modern art exhibits. I didn't even care that he got his choice. As we wandered past the paintings, I kept touching my bracelet.

My brain was in overdrive as I went back and forth, debating with myself whether or not the bracelet was real. It was hard to imagine.

But then again, humans going to the moon was hard to imagine, too, and our next stop was a museum filled with their space suits, rockets, and more. It was also hard to imagine that people actually painted the art we were looking at, especially since I could barely draw a straight line.

So maybe a magic bracelet could be real?

But, as Lucy, Addie, and Becca said, my wish had to be something great. Something amazing. Something I had always dreamt about.

The problem was, I had dreamt of so many things!

I wanted peace on earth.

I wanted to save the environment.

I wanted to protect the mountain gorillas, the orangutans, and the Asian elephants, all animals that could be extinct in the next decade.

I wanted to make sure everyone on the planet had enough food to eat and a roof over their head.

I also wanted an iPad.

And a chauffeur to take me to school.

And a bigger house with more bedrooms so I didn't have to sleep on Dadi's floor. Maybe a hotel. Could I wish for my own hotel? With a pool? And a hot tub?

I wanted Omar to be less annoying and Natasha to be less of a know-it-all. I wanted to be able to have shrimp pad thai or pizza whenever I wanted, and for there to be no more pranks.

There were too many choices.

How was I supposed to pick only one wish? Picking things was one of my least favorite things to do!

I hoped the wish offer didn't expire, because it was going to take me a while to choose the perfect life—and world—changing wish.

I followed my family into the west building. Dadi's face lit up as we looked at a giant painting of a bridge and lily pads.

"Can you imagine owning a gorgeous painting like this? By Monet himself? And getting to look at it every day?" she said with a laugh. "Maybe if I had millions of dollars."

Ooh. Back to the lottery idea. Or what if I wished for a million dollars? Two million dollars? A million for me and a million for Dadi. Or what if I wished for all the paintings in this hall to be mine? Or for the hall itself to be a wing in my own mansion?

"What's on your mind?" Dadi asked me as we left the museum. "You seem distracted."

"Oh, nothing," I said. As much as I wanted to tell Dadi everything, I knew she would be convinced the bracelet was some kind of scam and tell me to toss it. I've heard Dadi talk to some of the people who call the house and try to sell her things we don't need, and she can be fierce.

And I didn't want to toss the bracelet. I wanted to use my wish.

But for what?

"I'm excited for astronaut ice cream at the Air and Space Museum," I shared with Dadi instead. We're both big fans of the freeze-dried deliciousness sold at the gift shop. "We're going to get some, right?"

"Of course," she said. "It's out of this world."

I laughed, linked my arm through hers, and tried to push away thoughts of the bracelet, at least for now.

"What flavor will you get?" Dadi asked.

I sighed. Another decision to make.

After the museums, we came home and I checked my phone. The Best Wishes girls, as I'd started to think of them, had texted a bunch of times, asking me if I'd decided on my wish.

Me: **Not yet. I'm not good at making decisions, to be honest . . . 🙁**

Addie: Take your time!

Lucy: But not too much time! ⌛

Becca: Tell us before you do anything!

Me: kk. I'll decide tomorrow!

I could decide by then. Couldn't I?

4

In Charge

When I woke up on the air mattress Monday morning, I briefly forgot everything that had happened.

Then I saw the bracelet on my wrist.

I still hadn't picked a wish!

I'd had weird dreams all night. In one of them, I was flying. Like a bird.

Hmm. Did I want to wish that I could fly? Then I could get to school in two minutes! Although . . . I was kind of afraid of heights.

I got ready in a daze and ate my breakfast in silence while everyone chatted with Auntie and Sabrina about their plan to tour American University. I forgot to say thanks when I grabbed the lunch that Dadi gave me and was lost in thought for the entire bus ride to school. The bracelet and what to wish for were the only things on my mind throughout the whole morning.

"Maya!" Hazel nudged me during lunch, while I chewed on a carrot distractedly. "What's up? You're so out of it!"

Should I tell her?

Maybe she could help me pick a wish. Hazel was very good at being decisive.

But was telling her allowed? This magic bracelet felt like something that should be a secret from everyone except the Best Wishes crew.

Even my best friend. At least for now.

And, besides, what if Hazel convinced me to wish for something I didn't actually want? Hazel could be very persuasive.

Or what if she thought I was silly for believing in the magic?

"Maya!" Hazel repeated. "Can you hear me? What's going on?"

"Yeah, yeah. It's nothing. I'm fine," I said, touching the bracelet softly.

"Ooh. Nice bracelet," Hazel said, leaning over to peer at it. "Is it new?"

"Um, yeah, it was a . . . a gift," I said, pulling my sleeve over my wrist.

"From who?" Hazel asked.

From who? How would I even begin to explain that? I decided not to say anything. At least not yet.

"My aunt and cousin are visiting us," I said. That statement was true. I didn't say it was from them.

"It's pretty. So are you excited for environmental club today?" Hazel said. "I bought all this cool stuff that I'm bringing to the meeting."

“Yeah, sure,” I said. I was too distracted to think about the club at that point. I had to think of a wish!

“Did you see the posters and flyers I put up all over the school? My dad dropped me off early so I could get it done,” Hazel added. “Cassandra helped.”

“Oh, nice,” I mumbled. I was a little hurt that Hazel hadn’t asked me to help, but maybe it was because she knew I didn’t support the use of all that paper. Or maybe it was because I hadn’t returned her calls all weekend. I’d texted her only once to say that I was busy with family stuff.

When the final bell rang for the day, Hazel and I headed to the club meeting. Ms. Maxwell waved to us from behind her desk and Hazel stood in front of the room. I squeezed into the back row beside Leo, who I was happy to see had decided to join, along with a bunch of new people. I guessed all the flyers and signs had worked.

“Hi, everyone!” Hazel said. “Welcome to the second official meeting of the environmental club! I have so many fun updates. Who’s excited?!”

Everyone looked pretty hyped. Maybe this would be good after all?

“Since the club had a surplus club budget of a few hundred dollars from last year, I went to Target over the weekend and bought some great swag. Check out these cute sunglasses!" Hazel reached into the giant plastic bag she'd stashed by Ms. Maxwell's desk. She held up a pair of neon-green plastic sunglasses with the words *Warning: Global warming is HOT* printed on the sides.

Um . . .

"Everyone gets a pair!" Hazel squealed.

All the kids cheered like the sunglasses were the greatest thing they'd ever seen.

"And that's not all," Hazel continued. "I ordered a hundred helium balloons with the same slogan on them for our party! We can paint them with glitter so that they sparkle. They'll be so pretty floating up in the air!"

Everyone oohed and aahed when she held up a sample balloon.

"Hazel," I blurted out, a little louder than I'd planned.

Everyone turned to look at me. I felt my face warm up but I kept talking anyway.

"Plastic, balloons, and glitter are all . . . really harmful for the environment. Isn't the whole point of this club to do things to *help* the planet?"

It felt good to say that, and I saw a few people nodding.

"Of course that's the point of the club," Hazel replied.

"And part of helping the planet is getting people's attention and convincing them to care about it in the first place. Am I right?"

"Right!" a bunch of kids cheered again.

My cheeks burned. "But I don't think that this is the right way to go about it . . ." I protested, looking around for anyone who would back me up since it wasn't going to be my best friend. Leo had a little frown on his face, but I couldn't tell what he was thinking.

"Let's take a vote, then," Hazel said. "Whoever wants to move forward with my plans, say 'PARTY'!"

And just like that, the room erupted into a wild chorus of "PAR-TAY!"

I gulped hard, and my throat grew tight. Hazel and I usually saw things the same way. But I could tell she was enjoying her new role too much to listen to me.

"I'm not sure this is the best plan," Leo said to me in a quiet voice.

"It's not!" I agreed, grateful to have someone on my side. "It's the absolute worst."

He leaned his chair against the back wall. "I thought this club would be about action, like programs and cleanups and stuff."

"Exactly." I held up my notebook. "There are so many things we could be doing! Like composting. I came up with a whole system for it. And I have lots of other ideas for the club. I wish I was in charge!"

The words were barely out of my mouth when I felt a sudden blast of cold air fill the room. I shivered and looked around me, but no one else seemed to feel it.

A strange tingle in my limbs spread throughout my body. And then I noticed that the bracelet on my wrist was warm, and was it . . . *glowing* just a little?

Whoa.

I looked over at Hazel, who was still standing at the front of the room, holding up the balloon.

"Excuse me, everyone," Ms. Maxwell suddenly said, getting up from her desk. "I have an announcement."

"What is it, Ms. Maxwell?" Hazel asked.

"After some careful thought for the past minute," Ms. Maxwell declared, "I firmly believe that Maya Amir needs to lead this club."

* 5 *

Big Shot

I gasped.

What?

"Me? B-but why?" I sputtered.

Hazel looked stunned.

"Trust me," Ms. Maxwell said. "As club sponsor, I know what's best. Maya should be the leader. Hazel, if you wouldn't mind, I need you to go sit down. Maya, take it away."

Ms. Maxwell motioned for me to come to the front of the room.

Everyone turned to me and stared.

Oh, wow. What had just happened?

I was in charge of the environmental club?

I felt a surge of heat on my wrist. Why was my bracelet

glowing? What had I said? I'd been talking to Leo. I racked my brain to remember.

I'd said: "I wish I was in charge."

Speak one wish to make it true.

I had spoken my wish. Not on purpose. But I had spoken it! I had even used the word *wish*! And now . . . it was true!

I was in charge. Just like that.

Everyone was still staring at me. And then I stood up. I had to do something. I had to say something!

What should I say?

I walked to the front of the room and looked worriedly at Hazel. But she just shrugged and walked over to take my empty seat.

I faced the club members and cleared my throat.

"I . . . um . . . think . . . that . . . I think . . . that . . . we should return the sunglasses . . ."

Everyone continued to stare.

"And also the balloons . . ."

More staring.

"And the glitter . . . glitter makes a mess of everything, doesn't it?"

Some of the kids nodded.

"Maybe instead we can pick up garbage around the

school?" I said. "And we can . . . recycle it. Recycling is good! Let's do that. Does everyone want to do that? Or do you want to do something else? What do you want to do?"

More blank stares. Oh, wow. What was I even saying? How could I be in charge? I didn't know how to be in charge! I was never in charge of anything!

Leo raised his hand. "Maya, what about composting? You just told me that was something you thought our club could do?"

Right! Composting! I *had* just said that! "Yes, thank you!" I said, remembering. "Our school does a good job with recycling," I explained to the club, "but we put so much food in the trash. And that ends up in landfills. It would be much better for the environment—and even save the school money—if we started a composting program for all the food scraps. We could add a third bin beside the garbage and recycling in the lunchroom."

Everyone nodded and cheered. For me. And for composting. Wow. I grinned, feeling confident.

"What if people put the compost stuff in the wrong bin?" Hazel asked. She looked a little lost, and I didn't blame her. I hoped she wasn't angry at me.

"We would need . . . signs, I guess," I told her. "We

would definitely need signs. But! We're a green club. So we'll make the signs using paper from the recycling bin. Reuse, reduce, recycle."

Hazel cocked her head to the side and thought about it. "Good idea!"

"What do we do with the compost?" Cassandra asked me. "After it's in the bin."

"Hmm," I said. "Maybe we can start a hydroponic garden—a huge one! And then we can use the ingredients from the garden for school lunches. I think you can use compost for that. I'll have to ask my grandmother."

"That sounds like a great plan," Leo said, nodding at me approvingly.

"You're the best club president ever," a girl named Neda added.

I stole a quick glance at Hazel to see if she was upset by that comment, but she was smiling. I felt bad that I had stolen her job from her, but . . . my ideas *were* better.

When the club meeting was over, I waited for Hazel.

"So, you're not upset about me taking over?" I whispered to her.

Hazel's eyebrows furrowed.

"Should I be?" she asked.

"Um, no. I don't think so," I said.

"Okay." Hazel smiled at me. "Then I'm not."

"Great!" I smiled back, relieved. The magic must have worked on her, too.

So my wish had really come true. The bracelet was amazing.

The second I got home, I ran back to the laundry room and texted the Best Wishes group chat.

Me: It worked! It worked! IT WOOOOORKED

Becca: OMG tell us everything.

Addie: I guess you believe us now lol

Lucy: What did you wish for?!

I recapped everything that had happened in environmental club.

Me: It was a total accident! I didn't mean to make the wish! 🫣

Addie: I can't believe you took a chance wearing the bracelet when you weren't sure what you were going to wish for. Risky move, but I respect that!

Me: I wanted to be ready just in case. And it's fine! I ❤❤❤ my wish! I'm gonna do such cool stuff as president. And yeah, Hazel's my best friend but she was not the best president. She's good at leading, but her ideas were TERRIBLE. So I am happy with my wish.

Becca: It does seem like a great wish. And maybe you won't even have to take the bracelet off. Maybe you can just keep it on until the end of the school year.

Me: Oh! I can just STAY president.

Lucy: SOOOO excited for you.

Addie: Me too! Keep us posted! ☆

"Maya?" I heard Dadi calling. "Maya, where are you?"

I texted the girls that I had to go and went to go find my grandmother in the kitchen. "Yes, Dadi?"

She put her hand on my shoulder. "What should I make for dinner, meri jaan?"

"What do you mean?" I asked. I loved it when Dadi called me "my heart," but I wasn't ever consulted about food choices. Dadi asked my parents, and even Natasha and Omar sometimes, but never me. For me, when it comes to meals in this house, it's like preschool: You get what you get, and you don't get upset.

"I'm wondering what you think would be best," Dadi was saying. "Do you want me to make those noodles you like? Or butter chicken? Lamb biryani? Which one do you choose?"

Huh? Me?

"Um . . . lamb biryani sounds good. Maybe with some pakoras to start?" I figured if she was asking, I might as well try to get something Dadi only makes for parties or special occasions, since they take a lot of work.

She nodded. "Done. Great idea. And for dessert?"

Dessert, too? Amazing. We don't usually get dessert on weeknights. "How about some . . . gulab jamun?"

"Oh yes, my gulab jamun are excellent. Thank you, beti. Great choices! Our guests will love them."

I agreed. They *were* great choices. But why had Dadi asked me about the menu?

I felt the bracelet on my arm heat up.

Oh. Oh, wow. Did this have something to do with my wish, too? Was I in charge of the kitchen now?

I offered to help Dadi chop onions even though they make me cry.

"No, meri jaan, but maybe stay close by so you can sample the food and make sure it tastes good to you?"

"I'm sure anything you make will be good, Dadi," I told her. "I was thinking I should start my homework instead."

"Of course, of course," she said, shooing me away.

Since my room was still occupied, I settled onto the couch. I opened up my binder but couldn't think of anything other than the bracelet. I touched it and it was still warm. Finally, I took a deep breath and picked up my pencil. Why hadn't I wished for no homework for the rest of my life?

Just then, Baba came into the living room.

"Maya, what color should we paint the front of the house?" he asked, plopping down next to me.

"What?" I asked him.

For the past couple of weeks, I'd been hearing Baba and Mama talk about doing home improvements. I knew they'd hired a painter. But my parents never asked for my opinion on the topic. And that was fine with me, because I didn't have one.

Baba held up a swatch book with twenty different shades of beige. They all looked exactly the same.

"Which one do you like?" he asked me.

"I don't know," I said.

"I was thinking this one, called Misty Morning, but it has too much yellow in it. I really like Calming Breeze, but maybe it's a bit too gray," Baba continued, pointing to the little squares as he spoke.

"Okaaaay . . ." I said.

"So which one? Or do you think it should be something totally different? Like Tender Tentacles? Can you please choose? I need you to choose."

I started to sweat. I could tell Baba wasn't going to stop naming paint colors until I picked something. Anything.

"That one?" I said, pointing to Calming Breeze. "I mean, unless you think—"

"Perfect. That's settled! I knew you'd know what to do." Baba looked genuinely relieved, and it felt good to help him. Although now that I took a closer look, I was seriously wondering if Misty Morning was the better choice.

"Next we need to choose a welcome mat." Baba opened up a bunch of tabs on his phone and started showing me a dizzying selection of welcome mats. "What do you think? Once we pick this, we can move on to the porch lights."

All these questions were starting to stress me out. "Um . . ." I pointed my finger at a bright blue mat that said *welcome* in different languages. "That one?"

Baba nodded and clicked *buy*. Luckily, Dadi called us for dinner before we could get to the porch lights.

"Wow, what a spread!" Auntie said as we gathered around the table that Omar had set. "Look, Sabrina, there's pakoras. We haven't had those since Ramadan!"

"Enjoy," Dadi said, beaming. "Maya picked the menu."

"Wonderful!" my parents said. Even Natasha and Omar looked impressed.

We sat down and feasted on the meal. I've had Dadi's biryani a million times, but I swear this was the best one she's ever made. And then after dinner, as promised, she pulled out the nice bowls and brought over a tray of perfect gulab jamun floating in syrup. I didn't know how she did all that so quickly, but she's always been a wizard in the kitchen.

"To celebrate your visit," Dadi said to Auntie and Sabrina.

"Thanks, Ammi, what a treat," Mama said, her eyes wide with appreciation.

As we all dug into dessert, my mom turned to me.

"Maya, your father and I were thinking of changing investment companies. We might be able to get a higher return on our 401(k). What do you think?"

Now this was going too far.

"Me? Mama, I don't know anything about that!" I said, my heart hammering. "I think you need to ask someone else!"

"Maya, do you know any good restaurants around George Washington University?" Auntie asked. "Sabrina and I will be there tomorrow."

I focused on Auntie. I knew more about restaurants than whatever 401(k)s were.

"There's that pasta place near there that we went to once . . . um . . ."

"Cinque Terre?" Baba said.

"Yes! That one. And there's a really good muffin store . . ."

"JJ's Bakery!" Natasha said.

"Yes. Try those," I said, and Auntie wrote them down in her phone. I had to admit it felt good to have people finally be interested in what I had to say.

"Hey, Maya," Omar said. "I want to get the new version of *FIFA*. Do you think I should—"

"I'm trying to choose my classes for next year," Natasha interrupted, looking at me. "Do you think I should take AP History or Biology?"

"What college should I go to, Maya?" Sabrina asked me.

"I don't know!" I blurted out. "I don't know the answers to any of these questions!"

"What do you think about us opening a Roth IRA?" Mama asked me.

I quickly stood up. Being in charge was exhausting.

"Thank you for the delicious dinner, Dadi. I have to do my homework now, so please excuse me, everyone," I said firmly.

And then, my heart pounding, I locked myself in the laundry room until bedtime.

6
Head of the Class

The next morning, as I walked into my classroom, I had no idea what to expect. My wish was clearly working on more than just the club. So, what would that mean for the rest of school?

I took a deep breath as I sat down at my desk next to Hazel. I could—I would—handle whatever came my way.

"How was your night?" Hazel asked me.

"It was . . . a lot," I said.

"Did you work on more ideas for the club? Do you need any help?"

"Oh, um, no, I'm okay. Thanks." I felt weird asking her for help since I had, well, stolen her job.

"Good morning, students!" Principal Haig announced over the PA system. "Are you ready for a wonderful day? Today we're going to . . ."

As Principal Haig's announcements echoed throughout the classroom, I noticed Ms. Sokolov waving me up to her desk.

I stood up and tentatively approached my teacher. "Yes?"

"Maya, I have a question for you," she whispered, peering at me over her glasses. "Do you think the class is ready for their geography quiz?"

"Um, I'm not sure . . . ? Today?" I hadn't studied!

"Not today, but this week? Is tomorrow good or is that too soon? What do you think?"

I smiled to myself as I felt the bracelet heat up. Everyone, including my teacher, wanted to know what I thought about everything. But *this* question I could answer.

"I think . . . we don't need to have a quiz at all. Nobody likes quizzes. They're stressful," I told Ms. Sokolov.

She nodded. "I see your point. Forget it. Quiz canceled. Sound good?"

I nodded.

She nodded.

I nodded some more. "Okay if I go back to my seat now?"

She smiled. "Of course! Do whatever you want, Maya! My class is your class! What should we do today?"

"Can we . . . free read?"

"Great idea. Class, it's reading time!"

As I sat back down at my desk, I wondered—was that it? Or was she going to ask me my opinion on everything all day? Ooh. Maybe I could get rid of homework, too!

I was enjoying reading *The Last Mapmaker* when Ms. Sokolov stopped by my desk.

"Maya, would you mind taking a look at these short stories?" she asked. She dropped three papers onto my desk. They were our homework assignment from over the weekend. "I'm not sure about what grade to give them and was wondering what you think."

"You want me to grade"—I looked at the names and lowered my voice—"Cody's, Zara's, and Rachel's stories?"

"Yup! Thanks."

"Are you sure? I mean, I don't know if I can—"

"I'm sure you'll be great at being in charge of the grading." Ms. Sokolov smiled.

"If you say so . . ."

Ms. Sokolov walked back to her desk. I looked over at

Hazel to see if she thought it was weird that Ms. Sokolov had asked me to grade homework. But Hazel only shrugged and gave me a thumbs-up.

I put down my book and picked up Zara's story about a talking poodle. It was good. And funny. Since these were our creative writing assignments, I decided to focus on being kind and encouraging. I wrote one nice thing on each story. On Zara's I made a smiley face when the poodle said, "I had a ruff day." I fixed some of the capitalization on Cody's and Rachel's stories but also made lots of smiley faces.

So far, so good.

As soon as it was lunchtime, I hurried to the cafeteria with Hazel to see how the new composting bin was doing.

Hazel had written on the back of her other posters and flyers, explaining what to throw away where, and hung them up by the bins.

I peered into the composting bin and saw that some kids from the earlier lunch period—for first to fourth graders—had already used it. And properly! There were half-eaten sandwiches, apples with one bite taken out, and other unfinished snacks.

Hurrah.

"It worked!" Hazel said. "That was a great idea."

I smiled. Then I watched a fifth grader toss an empty milk carton into the composting bin. Oops. I reached into the bin and took out the carton, transferring it to the plastic recycling bin.

"Maybe I'll ask Principal Haig to let club members visit all the classrooms and explain the new system. We can help the kids who are still confused about where to put things," I said.

"Another great idea," Hazel said. "Building awareness is key. You're such a rock star!"

I beamed.

After we ate lunch, we went into the yard for recess. Hazel joined our classmates in a game of tag and I stood by the fence that faced the street, feeling pleased with myself. I was really good at being in charge! I was changing things for the better! Making the world a better place!

I smiled at the strangers walking by on the street.

A man pushing a stroller. An elderly couple holding hands. A woman in big sunglasses and a cream-colored coat. She wasn't walking, actually. She had stopped and was now staring at me.

Hmm. Did I know her?

The bell rang, and I went back inside, shrugging off the weird moment.

I was on my way to my desk when Ms. Sokolov waved me over again.

"Do you need me to grade more papers?" I asked.

"I actually need you to watch the class," she said, lowering her voice.

Wait, *what*?

"Are you getting coffee or something?" I asked.

"No." Ms. Sokolov picked up her blazer off the chair and

put it on. "I need to take off for a few hours. So, you're in charge."

My jaw dropped. "Take off? Like you're leaving school property?"

"Yup. No biggie. You can handle it." She gave me a big toothy smile.

I could? No, no, no! I couldn't! What did I know about running a classroom? "When are you coming back?!" I cried.

She grabbed her purse and slung it over her shoulder. "Tomorrow? I think."

"You think?! But . . . I can't be the new teacher!" My mouth felt dry, and my palms grew super sweaty. I really needed some water. And a towel.

"Of course you can. You are very capable! Everyone! Attention!"

The whole class looked up at us.

"Maya is in charge now, okay? Bye!"

And then she strutted right out of the classroom, leaving me standing by her desk.

Everyone stared.

Oh no. I gulped. I coughed. I blinked extra fast. What

was I supposed to do? I had no idea! I was now in charge of the entire class? There was no way this was allowed!

Everyone was still staring.

"Um. Hi? So . . . I guess I'm in charge now?" I looked around the room. No one else seemed to think it was strange that I was suddenly the teacher. "So . . . maybe we can . . . um . . ."

My voice trailed off. I felt kind of dizzy and held on to the desk for balance. What was I supposed to do with the class? What would a substitute do? I guessed I was kind of like a substitute. Except for being way too young and totally inexperienced.

"What, um, should we do today?" I finally asked the other kids.

Everyone started yelling different suggestions.

"Go outside!"

"Watch a movie!"

"Bake a cake!"

None of those seemed like realistic options.

"Play hide-and-seek!"

"Make a movie!"

"Stand on our desks!"

My heart raced. Oh no! Had I lost control of the class already? I needed to get it back. Quick.

I spotted Zara in the front row and thought of her clever story. Oh! Maybe I could give them a writing exercise?

"Okay, people! Quiet down!" I called.

No one heard me over all the shouting. Oh, wow. I had to do something dramatic, and fast. I stepped over to the light switch and flicked it on and off.

"Anyone who isn't quiet will go straight to the principal's office!" I called out in my most serious voice.

The class quieted down except for some grumbling.

"Now, take out your notebooks," I said. "The green ones."

Everyone took out their green notebooks. Well, almost everyone. There was still a little grumbling.

"I forgot mine at home!" Jeremiah said. "Or maybe my dog ate it?"

"I wanted to play hide-and-seek," muttered Benjamin.

"We're not playing hide-and-seek." I rolled my eyes. "And just use any piece of paper. With a pencil, I want you to write . . . a story."

"About what?" Leo asked. "Anything we want?"

"Um. No," I said. "I'm going to give you a writing

prompt. The prompt is . . . you wake up in the morning and there is a mysterious box with your name on it. You open the box and—that's the writing prompt." My voice was loud and clear.

"What's in the box?" Zara asked.

"Who sent it?" Cody asked.

"That's for you to decide!" I answered. "Now write for the rest of class. Then those of you who want to read your stories out loud can share. Now begin! Have fun! Best wishes!"

"Wishes?" Hazel asked.

"Never mind," I said. "Just write."

It turned out that teaching was a breeze.

Everyone in the class had a blast writing and a few kids even volunteered to share their work. When the final bell rang, the kids actually clapped for me for doing such a good job running the class. I floated out of school feeling like I could literally do anything!

When I got home, my whole family was waiting for me at the kitchen table.

"Maya, we need you to tell us what we should do for dinner," Dadi said.

This time, I was totally prepared.

"How about Founding Farmers? I could really go for some chicken and waffles." I glanced at my parents out of the corner of my eye. We hardly ever go to restaurants on weekdays, and Founding Farmers is more of a birthday treat kind of restaurant than a random Tuesday night place.

Dadi broke into a smile and said, "Yes, if that's what you want. I like their fish and chips."

And then my dad looked at my mom, raised his eyebrows, and said, "Why not?"

"Oh, that'll be nice," Mama agreed.

"No way!" Omar whooped. "Awesome!"

"I can do my homework later!" Natasha said.

"Sounds delicious," Auntie added.

"Do they have vegetarian options?" Sabrina asked.

And just like that, we were going to my favorite restaurant. Amazing! Being in charge was the best!

When we arrived at Founding Farmers, Baba asked for a table for eight.

"Let me see," the host said, scanning the seating chart. "I can put you over there in the back where it's quiet, or over here by the window. Which would you prefer?"

Everyone turned to me and waited for an answer.

"How about the window?" I said.

"Excellent, follow me," the host said.

We all sat at a big round table, and I didn't even need to look at the menu to know what I wanted to order. In most restaurants, I change my mind seven times before finally making a decision. But at Founding Farmers, I go straight for the chicken and waffles.

"Chicken and waffles, please," I told the waiter.

"One of the best things we have," he said. "That, and the pot pie."

"Should I get the pot pie?" Omar asked me.

"I don't know. You should get whatever you want."

"I'll get the pot pie," Omar said, nodding at me.

And, believe it or not, I was forced to pick everyone else's food for them. Luckily, I already knew what my family likes to order, but I'm not sure if Sabrina actually enjoyed her vegetarian quinoa bowl. (I was stuck deciding between that and the veggie burger.)

As we were eating, a woman came into the restaurant on her own. The place was pretty empty by then, but I saw her point to the table next to us. And then she sat down right behind me. She had blond hair and was wearing a cream-colored coat. She looked kind of familiar, but I couldn't place her. Maybe she was a celebrity? Or a politician I had seen on TV?

Mama's forehead crinkled up in confusion as she looked around at all the empty tables. She motioned toward the lady as if to ask us, *Why is she sitting there of all places?*

"Excuse me," the lady suddenly said to me. "I couldn't help but notice your bracelet. It's lovely."

"Thanks," I said, although something about her intensity was creeping me out.

"That *is* a nice bracelet," Sabrina said, peering over her bowl to get a better look. "Where'd you get it?"

"It was a gift," I said quickly, and then I put my arm under the table where no one could see it.

Just then a woman in a white coat and chef's hat came to our table.

"How is everything tasting?" she asked. Her name was printed on her jacket: *Chef Jackie.*

"Delicious!" we all said in unison.

"Would you like to see the kitchen? We're trying out some new items for the menu and would love your opinion," Chef Jackie continued. It sounded like she was talking to all of us, but she was looking directly at me.

"Um, sure," I said.

I followed the chef into the back. It was so cool to see the giant steel pots and pans and the staff chopping and stirring and assembling plates. It looked like a scene straight out of a movie.

"We're developing a trio of sauces for our signature steak," Chef Jackie told me, dipping a spoon into a saucepan. "What do you think of this?"

"Mmmm," I said politely after taking the tiniest taste. It was a little too salty for me.

"And this is our new chocolate mousse cake," Chef Jackie added, cutting off a small slice for me and handing me a plate.

That was more like it!

"Do you think we should serve it with a raspberry sauce or salted caramel?"

"What about . . . *both*?" I suggested.

Chef Jackie slapped her knee. "Why didn't we think of that?"

"Do you compost all these food scraps?" I asked when I noticed huge trash cans overflowing with uneaten food. "I'm starting a composting program at my school."

"Really? That's impressive. And it's definitely something we will look into! Thank you!" Chef Jackie said, beaming.

I happily tasted two more desserts, but when the host came back to the kitchen and started asking me for advice about the reservation policy, I said I needed to go back to my family.

To thank me, Chef Jackie sent over a tray of desserts for our whole table.

"Yum. Free is my favorite flavor!" Baba said.

I laughed and couldn't help but agree.

I looked over to see if the blond possible-celebrity had gotten a free tray of desserts, too, but she was gone.

Before going to sleep, I texted the Best Wishes girls.

Me: Hiiiii! Everything is still amazing!

Becca: Yay! 🎉

Addie: Go Maya!

Lucy: GREAT! What happened? Did you rule the club?

Me: More than just the club! My teacher left me in charge of the class! And then I kind of ran a restaurant!

Becca: 😱

Addie: No wayyyyy

Lucy: I would love to run a restaurant!

Me: It was so much fun!

Becca: Any sign of Eloise? Or did Lucy throw her off our scent for good?

Me: No sign!

Unless . . .

I thought back to the awkward blond lady at the restaurant.

Me: Wait. Does anyone have a picture of her?

Addie: Hold on, I do. She's on roller skates.

A second later, a picture of a blond lady came through. I froze. Oh no. It looked just like the woman at the restaurant! Wait. Was she also the person I had seen outside school? I think she was!

Me: Ugh. I actually saw her today. Twice.

Becca: Already??

Me: How did she find me?

Addie: She has a bead from the bracelet on her

neck. It's a tracker. It activates whenever the bracelet's magic is working.

Me: But what does that mean, "a tracker"?

Becca: I think it pulls her toward the bracelet?

Me: So it pulled her all the way to DC?

Lucy: Ask her when you see her again!

Becca: No, don't talk to her! Avoid her! She's bad news!

Me: She's definitely creepy.

Addie: So creepy.

Lucy: Let's get back to the good stuff then. The bracelet is fun?

I smiled. Then I wrote back:

Me: The bracelet is magical.

7

Rule the School

I wondered if Ms. Sokolov would be back the next day. But I didn't even make it all the way to my classroom before Principal Haig stopped me in the hallway.

"Maya, I need to talk to you," she declared.

"Okay," I said nervously. Was I in trouble? Was *Ms. Sokolov* in trouble for leaving me to run her classroom?

The principal put both hands on my shoulders. "I heard what a wonderful job you did running your class yesterday!"

Oh! "Thank you," I said. Phew.

"And, because you did such an excellent job, I need you to be in charge of school for the day."

"What?" I yelped in disbelief. "The whole school? Is that even allowed?"

"Yup!" Principal Haig said, turning to exit the school. "You're in charge. Use my office! Today it's your office! Good luck! Bye!" And then she was gone.

I looked down at my wrist. This bracelet was bonkers. Yes, I had wanted to be in charge of my club. And I hadn't really minded being in charge of my classroom. But being in charge of *the entire school*?

On the other hand, being principal for a day sounded . . . kind of awesome. It was just one day. I could do it! Plus, I had the magic of the bracelet. And clearly, the bracelet could do anything. I'd be fine.

I headed toward the office and waved to Mr. Witsky, the school secretary, who was at the desk in front.

I cleared my throat. "Um, so, I know this sounds weird, but I'm—"

"Principal for the day. I know!" he said. "Principal Haig told me. Thanks for filling in."

Like everyone else, he seemed to think it wasn't strange at all that I was suddenly in charge.

"No problem," I said. "Um, is there anything I should do?"

"You should probably do the morning announcements," he said.

Right! The announcements! "Got it."

"Also, there's some paperwork on your desk for you to sign."

"Are you sure my signature will be okay? You don't want to wait for Principal Haig to come back?"

"Yours is good," Mr. Witsky said with a nod.

Okay then. I headed over to the desk, hung my backpack over the chair, and rifled through the stack of papers that looked like they needed to be signed.

I don't really have an official signature, though I practice different ones sometimes for fun.

I signed one piece of paper. Then another. I even added a little heart at the end of my name because . . . why not? I signed another. Then another! I was a signing machine.

Done. Easy peasy! Now I just had to do the morning announcements.

"Um, anything specific I'm announcing?" I called to Mr. Witsky.

"The list is on your desk!"

Oh. Oops. I'd accidentally signed the announcements.

I picked up the paper labeled *Announcements* and

looked around. Then I yelled out, "How do I make the announcements?"

Mr. Witsky hurried into the office and pointed at the silver box on the side of the desk. There was a round button in the center. "Press that and talk."

Got it.

I pressed it and started to read.

"Good morning, students!"

My voice echoed around the room. "Are you ready for a wonderful day? We have an exciting morning and afternoon planned. The first graders are starting a new unit about kindness today. The second graders . . ."

I went on about all the grades, and the spaghetti and meatballs we were having for lunch, and then I decided to ad-lib:

"And we are so happy to tell you that our school is now composting in the cafeteria! So make sure to keep throwing all your food scraps into the bin! Save the planet!"

When I was done, I said thank you and pressed the button.

"Woot!" I cheered.

"Woot" echoed around the room.

Oops. "How do I turn this off?" I asked Mr. Witsky.

"How do I turn this off?" echoed around the room.

"Press the button twice," Mr. Witsky said.

I pressed the button twice. The light went out. Done!

Finally, I could relax. School was in session. Classes were happening. I put my feet up on the principal's desk and smiled.

Knock, knock.

One of the third-grade teachers was at my door.

"Can I help you?" I asked, quickly removing my feet from the desk.

"Sorry to bother you," she said, "but the custodian asked me to come and get you. We're having a problem in the teachers' lounge."

"Oh, sure," I said, jumping out of my chair.

I followed the teacher up the stairs to the second floor. I was so excited! I'd never been in the teachers' lounge before! No kid had! It was for teachers only. Who knew what they even did in there? Besides lounging. My heart was thumping with excitement.

I opened the door carefully. Ooooh. It was just as wonderful as I expected. There were couches. And a television. And a mini kitchen! With a box of donuts on the counter for anyone to take. Yum. Best lounge ever!

Maybe we could have our environmental club meetings in here from now on!

"What's the problem?" I asked the third-grade teacher as I helped myself to a donut with sprinkles. "Everything looks great."

"It's in the bathroom," she said.

I put down the donut and followed her to the single bathroom in the back of the lounge. I looked inside and saw the custodian furiously plunging the toilet. Water was spilling over onto the floor. Gross!

"Thank goodness you're here. I need your help!" the custodian said.

Uh-oh.

"Help doing what?"

"Plunging! You plunge, I'll adjust the water." He handed me the plunger and said, "Ready, set, plunge!"

I gingerly held the plunger with my fingertips. I hadn't done this before.

"Just place it over the hole in the toilet and press down," the custodian explained. I held my breath and plunged. He adjusted the water.

The water kept gushing into the toilet bowl. And out of the toilet bowl. My sneakers grew soggy.

"Plunge harder!"

I plunged harder. Was it working? Ahhhh!

One day on the job and I was going to break the toilet in the teachers' lounge!

"Almost got it!" the custodian said, and then finally the water level started to go down in the toilet bowl. It was working! I was sweating, and my arms were killing me, but we were doing it!

"BRRRRRRRRIIIIIIIIIIIIIIIIIIIIIIIING—"

Startled, I dropped the plunger. "What was that?"

"The fire alarm," the custodian said.

"BRRRRRRRRIIIIIIIIIIIIIIIIIIIIIIIING—"

"Oh no! I have to go!" I yelled. I wasn't sure where I was supposed to go, but I figured I had to help the rest of the school.

"But the toilet! We're not done yet!"

"I'll come back for the toilet," I said, and ran out of the teachers' lounge. Where was the fire? What was I supposed to do?

"BRRRRRRRRIIIIIIIIIIIIIIIIIIIIIIIING—"

My heart raced. All the kids were streaming out of their classes. But not fast enough. And I was in charge. One day on the job and I was going to burn down the whole school. This was all on me!

"Hurry!" I yelled. "Let's go, let's go!"

I needed to get everyone out of here as fast as possible.

"Let's go, let's go!" I repeated. I had to save the kids! And the teachers! I needed to save everyone!

"MOVE FASTER!" I shouted. "Everyone outside. Hurry, hurry!"

Mr. Witsky was standing at the door of the office. "Why are you not hurrying?" I asked him.

"It's a drill," he said calmly.

"It is? Why didn't you warn me?"

"There was a memo on your desk!"

I sighed. I guess I'd signed that, too.

The day continued to spiral more and more out of control.

At eleven o'clock, Ruby, the fourth grade's pet gerbil, escaped.

The teacher asked me to help search for Ruby. I looked in the kindergarten wing, the art room, and the equipment room next to the gym. But she wasn't anywhere.

Then, at first lunch, there was another gross problem: the

composting bin was totally overflowing. And it stank.

"What are you going to do?" the lunch lady asked me. "Where does the composting go?"

"Um . . . somebody has to take it away," I said.

"The trash collection people?" she asked. "Or the custodian? Somebody mentioned creating a hydroponic garden. Do we put it there?"

I realized that I'd forgotten to ask Dadi how the composting and garden worked.

I wasn't sure what to do. I really could use some advice from Dadi. Or Hazel. Or anyone else. But I was supposed to be the one in charge!

"Ahhhhhhhh!" a kid suddenly screamed. "A rat!"

She pointed at a small brown animal as it scurried under a table.

Was it a rat? Or was it Ruby?

As the rat/Ruby ran through the kids' feet, a wave of screams and shrieks went through the lunchroom.

Until the rat/Ruby got to the kindergarten table.

It jumped right onto the table and looked a tiny red-headed boy in the eye. I breathed a sigh of relief.

It *was* Ruby.

Then the boy started to shriek. Everyone started to shriek.

Then everyone started to run.

To the doors, to the windows, across the room.

“What is happening?” the lunch lady asked.

“I don’t know.” It was total chaos.

One of the kindergarten kids started bawling.

“Waah!” another kid wailed, his face turning bright red.

And then the kid sitting next to the wailer started screaming, “Mommmmmmy!”

And then . . .

They all started crying and screaming.

“I want my mommmmmmy!”

“I want my daddy!”

“Bubbie!”

“Binky!”

Their faces were covered in tears and snot. One kid lay down on the ground and started kicking his legs in a full tantrum. What was I supposed to do?

“You have to stop this!” the lunch lady told me.

“Me?” I asked. “How?”

“You’re in charge!”

But maybe I didn’t want to be!

I looked down at my bracelet, which was still glowing on my wrist. I wanted it off. Right now. I was done with being in charge. I tried to slide it over my hand, but it got stuck. Why was there no clasp? There had to be a way to get this off!

"You have to do something," the lunch lady told me.

Yes—I had to stop the magic.

But how? I tried to push the bracelet off my wrist again. But it didn't fit over my hand. There was no way I was getting this off here.

The chaos continued and there was nothing I could do to stop it.

"That sounds awful. At least no one threw up," Becca said over FaceTime.

"Throw-up *is* gross," Lucy said. "I had to deal with vomit every day when I was stuck in a time loop. Stupid yogurt."

"I threw up a lot of banana pie because of my wish," Addie sighed. "A lot."

"There was no throw-up," I said. I was hiding in the laundry room on FaceTime with Lucy, Addie, and Becca. "But a few kids did pee themselves."

"Yikes," said Becca. "I had a messy cafeteria, but thankfully no pee."

"It was bad," I sniffed.

"So then what happened?" Addie asked.

"Well, the crying set off a chain reaction . . ."

"Oh no," Lucy said.

"Oh yes," I said. "And then all the little kids were covered in snot, and crumbs, and probably pee! I had to send them to the nurse's office to get cleaned up. And we had to send the whole kindergarten class home. And I couldn't fix the toilet . . . so that was more pee. And then I saw a rat. In the compost bin. But I wasn't sure if it was the gerbil again."

"Gross!" Addie cried.

"I know. I had to call a pest control company. And a plumber. And after I told the first graders they could play volleyball, I had to call a glass window repair company. And when I was answering emails, I think I sent a computer virus to the other teachers—"

Becca whistled.

"It was bad," I admitted.

"Wow," said Addie.

"Is the principal back tomorrow?" Lucy asked.

"She better be!" I said, my heart racing. "I can't do this again."

"You might have to," Becca said.

"Can't I just take the bracelet off?" I asked, tugging on it once more. It didn't budge.

"No," all three of them said in unison.

"But . . ."

"No," they repeated.

"Not until it's ready to come off," Addie said.

"I'm ready for it to come off right now . . ."

A text popped through from Hazel:

You did a great job today! Can't wait to see what you do tomorrow! Here to help with the club if you need an extra set of hands! 🙌

The magic was *really* strong if she thought I'd done a great job.

Me: Thank you! I don't need help but thank you!

"Maya!" I heard Dadi call. "Where are you?"

Wait. I suddenly remembered something. "I have to go, I'll call you later," I said to the Best Wishes girls, and hit the end button. I grabbed the phone and rushed out of the laundry room. Dadi would be able to get this bracelet off. Even if the other girls couldn't figure it out, they didn't have Dadi! I remembered the time my Eid bangles were a little too tight and my grandmother showed me how to use soap and squeeze my hand tight to slip them on and off. She could do that again for me now!

"Maya," Dadi began, "do you think—"

I cut her off and showed her my wrist. "Dadi, I need you to get this off me. Like you did with the Eid bracelets. Remember?"

Her face crinkled. "Hmm. I can try. This is very unique looking. Where is it from?"

"Um . . . it was a gift."

"Let's go to the sink."

She covered my wrist with suds and made the water warm. Then she squeezed my hand firmly, like she was folding it in half, and tried to slide the bracelet off. But it wouldn't budge.

Dadi frowned and pulled a pair of scissors from the junk drawer. "I can try to cut it off."

"Go for it."

I winced while she carefully tried to cut it. But that didn't work, either.

The bracelet was still very much on my wrist.

"What a strong metal. Just leave it on, it's nice," Dadi said. "Meanwhile, what did you decide on for dinner?"

Why did I have to decide everything? "I don't know . . ."

Suddenly, my dad, my mom, and my brother were in the bathroom, all crowding around me by the sink.

"Maya, I need your help—"

"Maya, do you think—"

"What should I—"

"I'm wondering if—"

Noooo. I could not deal with them right now. I wanted to cover my ears like one of those kindergartners and scream. *Biiiiiinky!*

"I need a break!" I barked. I needed air.

I slunk out into the living room and headed straight for the front door.

I closed it behind me and took a deep breath. Ahh. Quiet.

I heard the creak of a branch.

I looked around and saw . . . Eloise.

She was standing behind one of our bushes, in full creep mode.

"Hello," she said, smiling in a super-fake way. "I didn't mean to startle you. I'm—"

"Eloise!" I called out. "It's you! Perfect! I am so glad to see you!"

She blinked multiple times. "Oh! Wow!" she said. "I wasn't expecting you to know who I am. Or to want to see me . . ."

I took the porch steps two at a time and ran right up to her. "Take the bracelet! Right now! Go for it! It's all yours! I don't want it!"

She leaned toward me eagerly. "It's off?"

"No, it's not off! It's still working! That's why I want you to take it! I don't want it! It's terrible! Take it, take it, take it!"

She took a step back. "I can't get it off for you," she said nervously.

"Why not?"

"I've tried. I don't know how to get it off. I can only take it once it's off your wrist."

I wanted to scream, *Ah, what good are you?* but I didn't. I just frowned.

"I'm sorry, I wish I could do more," Eloise said. "But I am glad we are on the same page. Maybe I can try something tomorrow . . ." Her eyes lit up. "A blowtorch? I bet I could burn right through it . . ."

Yikes. Now I took a step back. "Um . . ."

"I know exactly where to get one, no problem. I'll have your bracelet off in thirty seconds."

"Hold on there," I said nervously. "I want the bracelet off, not my arm. Can you think of something a little less scary?"

"It'll only hurt for a second," she said quickly. "If at all . . ."

"Think of something else," I ordered.

She took her phone out of her purse. "Let me check what time the hardware store around here opens . . ."

"No blowtorch," I said in my most forceful voice, and turned back to my door.

My entire family had their faces pressed against the window, waiting for me.

"You have to go," I told Eloise.

"See you tomorrow," Eloise said. "I'll get it off somehow, don't you worry."

I was worried. But I wanted it off.

I stepped back into my house and everyone crowded around me again, asking questions.

"Maya! Do you think—"

"Maya! I'm wondering—"

"Maya! Can you help me—"

I was suddenly exhausted.

"Time for bed," I announced. "Everyone. Please go to your rooms. Good night!"

I went straight to my blow-up mattress on Dadi's floor. I didn't even have the energy to call back the Best Wishes crew. I was too tired.

But maybe the magic was getting tired, too. Maybe it would wear off by morning.

I wished.

8

Follow the Leader

The next morning, the bracelet was still on, tight as ever.

I lay on the air mattress with the covers pulled over my head. Maybe if I just stayed here, on the floor in Dadi's room, on my half-deflated air mattress, out of sight, no one could ask me to be in charge of anything.

I know, I know. It wasn't the greatest plan in the world, but it was the best idea I could come up with at seven a.m.

"Maya! Get up! You're going to be late!" Dadi called from downstairs.

I stayed quiet, pretending to be asleep.

"Omar, go get her!" I heard Dadi say. "She needs to tell me what to make for breakfast."

I groaned and pulled the covers around me, wrapping myself up tight like a mummy. I didn't want to choose breakfast. Eggs, pancakes, waffles, toast. There were so many . . . choices. Ugh. I just wanted Dadi to pick, like she used to.

Omar appeared in the doorway.

"Dadi wants you," he said.

"I don't feel good," I grumbled. "I can't move."

"What's wrong? Do you want me to take your temperature? Do you want to go to the doctor? Should I call an ambulance?" I could hear the worry in Omar's voice. Why was he so worried?

"I don't feel that bad," I said, and then I poked my head out of the blanket. "I'm just really tired."

"Oh." Omar sounded relieved. "That's good. Because I need you to choose a topic for my history project. I was thinking of researching samurai or maybe the ancient Silk Road. What do you think?"

I moaned.

"It's too early to think, Omar. You pick."

Just then my mom and dad came into the room. Mama was holding two shirts and Baba was holding his razor.

"Good morning, Maya," Mama said. She held up a frilly

blouse with a tie around the neck and a striped button-down. "Which one of these should I wear?"

"Do you think I should go back to a goatee or stick with this beard?" Baba asked me.

I pulled the covers over my head again as I heard Natasha coming into the room. "Maya, do you like this nail polish?" she asked frantically.

Everyone was crowding around me.

"Maya, Maya!" my mom said.

"Why aren't you getting up?" Baba asked.

"We need you!" Omar and Natasha cried at the same time.

"I'm not going to school today!" I declared. I figured that if I was in charge, I should at least be able to decide that much, right?

Everyone spoke at once.

"But why?"

"Are you okay?"

"What's the matter?"

I could see the concern on their faces and it made me feel guilty. But not guilty enough to get up.

Just then Dadi walked into the room holding her phone to her ear. She looked confused when she saw me still lying on the air mattress and everyone standing over me. But she continued to speak into the phone.

"Oh yes, Farida, I can't even begin to tell you, our Maya is so talented, mashallah! Can you believe they made her *principal* of her school? Yes! As a fifth grader! Not president of the class, not president of the students, but in charge of the entire school! I mean, of course, we always knew she was special, but we didn't know that this was even possible! Since she was a baby, I knew she took after . . ."

Dadi went on and on bragging to her best friend, telling her how amazing I was. Ughhh! It just made me feel worse.

My family didn't understand how incredibly terrible everything had been yesterday. I was a total disaster!

"Oh yes, with this on her résumé, there will be so many good opportunities ahead of her, inshallah! And for college! And yes, yes, we are just so proud," my grandmother continued to say as she motioned for everyone to get out of the room. My parents, Natasha, and Omar grudgingly left.

Dadi would have been much better than me at being in charge of everything.

I went to the bathroom and took an extra-long time brushing my teeth.

I stared at myself in the mirror.

"What did you do, Maya?" I said to the girl in the reflection. She looked as scared and overwhelmed as I felt.

"OMG, MAAYYYYYYYAAAAA!" I heard Omar yell from downstairs. "You better come down here! The police are outside!"

Yeah, sure. Sounded like a typical Omar prank to me. I spat out my toothpaste. "I don't have time for this, Omar!"

"I'm serious! You have to come right away!" I could hear the alarm in his voice.

I ran out of the bathroom and downstairs.

"What? What is it?" What now?

Omar was jumping up and down as he pointed out the window.

"Look!" he shouted.

A bunch of police cars and police officers on motorcycles, all with flashing lights, were pulling up in front of our house.

OH NO!

Had they found out about the magic bracelet?

How?

Had someone from school tattled on me?

Hazel, maybe? Leo?

Or had Eloise called them?

But what had I done wrong?

Had I broken some kind of law?

I started to sweat.

Behind the police cars were a bunch of big black cars with tinted windows.

THIS IS BAD.

I'M IN REALLY BIG TROUBLE!

"Do you see . . . those . . . flags?" Omar was gasping for

air as Dadi, Natasha, and I huddled around the window, looking outside. "Do . . . you . . . know . . . what . . . that . . . means?"

I squinted in the bright light and saw an American flag and another navy blue flag waving in front of a couple of the black cars.

I gulped.

I wasn't sure what all this meant, other than this looked like serious business. *Very* serious business.

At that moment, a man and a woman, each in black suits and dark sunglasses, got out of one of the vehicles. They were both wearing earpieces.

KNOCK! KNOCK! KNOCK!

We all jumped at the sound of the door, even though we had just watched them walk up to the house.

"I'll get it!" Dadi said, looking fearless as she adjusted her dupatta over her hair. She was still holding a spatula and I found myself wondering what she was planning to make for breakfast. Would I even get to eat it?

"Can I help you?" Dadi asked the people in the suits and sunglasses.

"We're looking for Maya Amir," the woman said.

I gulped again.

"What for?" Dadi's tone was challenging, and she narrowed her eyes.

"Ma'am, we need you to step aside," the man said.

"How dare they!" Dadi grumbled in Urdu to the rest of us. "They can't talk to me like that in my own house!"

I felt a shiver of fear at the idea of Dadi trying to protect me with the spatula and getting arrested, all because of my wish. So, even though my heart was beating so hard I was certain everyone could hear it, I stepped forward.

"Here I am," I said as calmly as I could, although I was afraid I was going to throw up.

"Maya Amir?" The woman nodded at me. "We need you to come with us. It's a matter of national priority!"

I looked down at my pajamas.

"Can I at least change my clothes first?" I asked, my voice tiny.

"There's no time for that. Get in the car. We will provide you with everything you need," the man said.

"Who are you? What is the meaning of this?" Baba came running downstairs with his face lathered up with shaving cream and half his beard missing.

“You can’t take our daughter!” Mama shrieked, following behind him.

Dadi turned to them and held up her spatula.

“I’ll stop them,” she said in Urdu.

“No, no, it’s fine,” I quickly said. “Don’t worry. I’m pretty sure I know what this is about. I’ll just talk to them real quick, and everything will be okay. Trust me.” I sounded way more convinced of this than I felt.

Then, before anyone in my family could stop me, I took a deep breath and followed the man and woman out of the house. I held my head high and ignored all the nosy neighbors who were standing on their porches or peeking out their front doors. When we got to the biggest car, the man opened the door for me and stepped aside, like I was some kind of celebrity.

I took a look back at my parents, who seemed frozen with fear, and tried to smile at them to reassure them. Whatever happened next, I was going to have to fix this myself.

And then I slid onto the soft black leather seat.

When I looked up, I was face-to-face with the president of the United States.

I rubbed my eyes and pinched the skin on my hand to make sure I wasn't dreaming. Then I looked down at my bracelet and saw it was still glowing slightly and warm to the touch.

"Hello, Maya," the president said to me. He cleared his throat and then leaned closer to me before saying, "I need you to be in charge."

* 9 *

Hocus POTUS

My jaw dropped. "Of what?"

"What do you mean 'of what'?" he asked. "Of the country! What else?"

"You want me to be in charge OF THE COUNTRY? Of the United States of America? You want me to be the leader of the nation, our nation? Are you kidding me?" I knew that I was talking to the president, and it felt weird to be so blunt, but I couldn't stop myself.

"Would I joke about something like this?" he asked, his eyebrows pulled together in confusion.

"I don't know you well enough to know the answer to that!" I said, being perfectly honest.

"Well, no. I am not joking. I need you to take over for a

little bit." The president smiled, like he was perfectly comfortable with this arrangement. Even if this wasn't a joke, and was happening because of the magic, I couldn't help but wonder: Was he feeling okay? Because this was taking things way too far. I mean, who in the world would think that asking a fifth grader to be president of the United States was acceptable?

"But I am *not* a good leader," I explained. "Yesterday, I was in charge of my school and I pretty much broke it. I don't want to break the country next."

"Don't look at it that way—I'm sure something positive happened," the president said reassuringly. "Would you like something to drink? I've got sparkling water and lemonade back here. And don't tell the First Lady, but there's a secret stash of cookies."

"They had to call a pest control company," I said flatly, refusing the drink and cookies with a wave of my hand. "And a plumber. And a glass repair guy—"

"Well, thank you for hiring small businesses," he said. "You helped the economy."

"I guess." I hadn't thought of that. "But I also had to send an entire class of kindergartners home."

"They must have loved that! I bet it boosted your approval ratings."

"There was pee involved."

"When you gotta go, you gotta go," he said.

"But I don't have—"

The president stretched his arms behind his head. "It's all good. Listen, this presidency is a bigger job than I thought it would be. I need your help. Our country needs your help."

"But—"

Suddenly, there was a rap on the car window that startled us both.

I looked through the tinted window. It was Dadi!

"Do you know her?" the president asked.

"Yes," I said. "She's my grandma. You better open it."

The president rolled down his window.

Dadi stood in front of us, her hands on her hips. Her dupatta was flapping in the breeze and her eyes were fierce. She was still in her fuzzy bedroom slippers. Luckily, the spatula was nowhere in sight.

"Where do you think you're going?" she asked.

"To the White House," the president said.

"You are not taking my Maya anywhere alone," Dadi said in her most commanding voice. "No way. I'm coming with her."

The president shrugged. "Sure, why not. Come on in."

And then just like that, he opened the door and my grandmother slowly slid herself inside, beside me. "All good?" he asked her.

She nodded, looking around the interior of the car. For once, Dadi seemed too stunned to say anything else.

He nodded back. "Then let's go."

I looked out the back window as we started driving away.

The rest of my family was standing on my porch.

My neighbors were on *their* porches.

And behind us, standing on the sidewalk, was Eloise, looking absolutely shocked by this turn of events.

Which was kind of how I felt.

Also she was holding a blowtorch. Yes, an actual blowtorch.

I shivered and sank into my seat.

As we drove along, Dadi whispered to me, "Do you think this is the *real* president or a body double? I heard they all have body doubles."

The president could totally hear her.

"Ma'am, I assure you, I'm the real president."

Dadi took out her phone and called my parents to tell them that everything was okay. She started to invite them to join the motorcade in our minivan and meet us at the White House, but the president cleared his throat loudly.

"Okay, maybe later, I'll let you know," she quickly added. "I have to call Farida! She won't believe this. Her grandson may be going to medical school, but how many people can say—"

"I'm afraid I'm going to have to stop you there," the president cut in. "We are going to keep this whole thing confidential, on a need-to-know basis only. Am I clear?"

"Okay, I got it," Dadi said, looking sheepish. Bragging to Farida Auntie was going to have to wait until later.

We pulled up to the White House and Dadi took my hand and squeezed it tight. I could hear her mutter the familiar prayers that she constantly makes under her breath for safety and strength, and I started to make my own, too.

Someone opened up the car door for us and we followed the president into the building.

I stepped into the red-carpeted hall with massive columns and marble statues and tried not to freak out. I was in the actual WHITE HOUSE! For the first time ever!

"This is the entrance hall," the president said like a tour guide. "It's where we receive official guests. Please, look around and get settled, and I'll see you later."

A woman in a black suit and a tight bun smiled at me like I wasn't a regular kid wearing pink pajamas with sheep all over them and said, "Welcome, Miss Amir. I'm Alessandra. I'll be assisting you today. First, let me show you and your grandmother where you'll be staying and where you can get ready."

Dadi and I were still holding hands as we followed Alessandra, who walked so quickly down the hallway that we struggled to keep up with her. We passed more statues and paintings and peeked into fancy rooms. It felt like we were moving through a museum.

"The White House is six levels," Alessandra said. "It has one hundred and thirty-two rooms, thirty-five bathrooms, twenty-eight fireplaces, and three elevators. It also has a chocolate shop, a private movie theater, and a bowling alley."

"Wow," I said. I love chocolate. I love movies. I really love bowling.

Finally, Alessandra stopped and opened the door to a beautiful bedroom with two big canopy beds, blue-and-gold curtains, and a fireplace with a sofa and chair in front of it.

"Amazing," I said, catching my breath. "This is all . . . wow."

Dadi walked in and touched the petals on the red, white, and blue roses in a gigantic vase on an ornate carved table.

"They're real!" she said. "Very nice."

"They're from the White House flower garden," Alessandra said. She walked over to a closet and opened it. Inside was a row of suits in different colors, a lot like the one she was wearing.

"Please dress in any of these that you like, Miss Amir. And in the bathroom you'll find all necessary toiletry items. I'll be back in a bit, unless there's anything else you need?"

"There is one thing," I asked. "Could I maybe get an . . . iPad? I'll give it back when I leave. But I forgot my mom's old phone at home."

Dadi had wandered over to a table where there was a big spread of breakfast: eggs, pastries, jams, and a white-and-gold teapot with the presidential seal on it. She inspected everything carefully.

"And some hot milk for my tea, please? With cardamom?" Dadi asked as Alessandra opened the door to leave.

"Absolutely," Alessandra said.

I started to look through the suits, which were all my size. I was deciding which color to wear when there was a knock on the door.

A butler appeared holding an iPad and handed it to me.

"This is a secure device," he said.

"And my things?" Dadi started to say as he held out a tray with a tiny pitcher of milk and a crystal bowl with the cardamom pods she'd asked for.

Now *that* felt like magic! Dadi was impressed.

I quickly picked the navy blue suit with a cream blouse and some brown shoes. I couldn't help but feel like an impostor. I looked in the mirror and saw a kid playing dress-up. Dadi twisted my hair into a bun. I looked nice, but hardly presidential.

When I was done getting dressed, I FaceTimed Lucy from the bathroom while Dadi had her tea. Luckily, I remembered her contact info.

Lucy was eating a bowl of oatmeal and smiled when she saw me.

"Why are you dressed like that?"

"You won't believe this. Can you quickly add in the others?"

Addie was walking out her front door when she picked up and said hi.

Becca was at her locker at school, cupping her phone for privacy.

"What's up?" she whispered.

"You're not going to think this is real, and I'm not even supposed to tell you, so don't tell anybody else, but—"

"Trust me, we'll believe anything," Lucy interrupted.

"I'm at the White House."

"The ACTUAL White House?" Addie gasped.

"Yes. The actual White House."

"No way!" Becca whisper-yelled.

"What for?" Lucy whispered.

I quickly explained about the motorcade showing up

and my conversation with the president and how I now had my own room with a bunch of suits.

My three new friends all freaked out at various volumes.

"So what does this mean?" Addie asked. "Are you, like, the vice president now?"

"I don't know what is happening," I said as I rubbed some of the official White House scented lotion into my hands. "He said he wants me to be in charge, but . . . he can't really mean that! Not after what happened at school yesterday—"

"Everything will be okay!" Lucy said in a louder voice than before.

"You got this!" Addie added.

"You can do anything," Becca agreed. "We're here for you if you need us!"

"Yeah, I'll totally come to the White House!" Lucy said.

"Can we have a sleepover?" Addie asked.

"Do you get to meet the presidential puppy?" Becca asked.

I heard another knock on the door.

"Gotta go!" I said nervously. "Wish me luck!"

When I went back into the room, Alessandra was standing there with an iPad of her own.

"The president would like to see you in the Oval Office at 10:04," she said.

"That is a very specific time," I said.

She nodded. "Every minute counts here."

Dadi handed me a croissant filled with butter and jam and said, "You need to eat this—it is the best croissant I've ever tasted."

I grabbed it and followed Alessandra out the door.

∗ 10 ∗

Power Trip

At exactly 10:04 we stood outside the door to the Oval Office.

"He said you should go on in," Alessandra told us.

"Shouldn't we knock?" I asked.

"Nope. He's expecting you."

So I opened the door. I had my iPad with me but nothing else. I wasn't sure what I needed. A pencil? A binder? A degree in political science?

"Hello?" I said. "Anyone here?"

"Hellooooooo," Dadi repeated.

The Oval Office looked exactly as it did in the movies.

It was big. It had high ceilings. It was oval. There were flowery beige couches facing each other with a small table between them. And a big royal blue carpet spread across the floor. There were a few sculptures of heads, a few flags, lots of paintings, and long yellow window drapes. There was also one brown, gleaming wooden presidential desk. And a fancy-looking swivel chair behind the presidential desk.

But there was no one sitting on the fancy chair.

"Mr. President?" I asked. "Are you here?" He wouldn't be hiding under the desk, would he? No, my brother would do that, but not the president.

"Let's sit and wait," Dadi said, sinking into one of the couches. "I'm sure he'll be around in a second. This couch is comfortable. And look, he left us cookies!"

There was indeed a plate of cookies on the coffee table. The president really likes his cookies.

"Do you think we're allowed to sit and snack?" I asked.

"Of course," she said. "Why would there be a couch if we weren't supposed to sit on it? Why would there be cookies if they weren't supposed to be eaten? No one leaves out cookies for decoration."

She had a point. So I sat on the other couch, facing her.

I took a cookie.

"But don't get crumbs on the cushions," she said.

I took a cloth napkin as well.

"He did say to be here at 10:04, right?" I asked, glancing at the grandfather clock across from me as I munched. It was now 10:07.

"Maybe he meant 10:40," Dadi said, taking a bite of her cookie. "That would be a more normal time to say. Or 10:45. Who says 10:04?"

"Someone whose minutes are very important."

"Everyone's time is important," she sniffed. "He has no problem wasting ours."

"At least he left us cookies," I said. "They're really good. Gooey. I bet they're from the chocolate shop. Maybe we should go bowling while we wait?"

The clock continued to tick. We continued to wait.

"This is ridiculous," Dadi sniffed twenty minutes later.

"Maybe he's operating on Desi Standard Time," I joked.

"Hah." Dadi smirked.

Suddenly, my iPad rang. I flipped it over.

Call from: The president of the United States.

Was this for real?

I clicked the accept button.

"Hello?"

The screen filled with the president's face. He was wearing sunglasses, a baseball hat, and a big grin.

"Hey there, Maya!" he said. "How's it going?"

"Is that him?" Dadi huffed. "Where is he?"

He definitely wasn't in the Oval Office. Instead of the suit he'd been wearing this morning, he was wearing a blue . . . swim shirt? Wait. Was that sand behind him? Was he sitting on a beach chair?

"Mr. President! Where are you?" I asked. "That doesn't look like the White House."

He cleared his throat. "I am not permitted to disclose my exact location, I'm afraid."

"But . . . are you at a beach? It looks like you're at a beach," I said.

"He's at a beach?" Dadi tsked.

The president cocked his head. "I am afraid I can't confirm or deny if I'm at a beach."

I heard a wave crash in the background.

"You are definitely at a beach!" I cried. "And you're supposed to be here!" I motioned around the room. "In the Oval Office!"

Dadi sighed. "I bet he's in Miami. Or maybe Montecito with Oprah."

"I can't confirm or deny if I'm with Oprah," the president said.

Dadi's eyes lit up. "He's with Oprah!"

"You're supposed to be with me! Here!" I yelled.

"I know, I know. But you see, I desperately needed a break. Being president is exhausting! There is so much to do. Every minute is scheduled! And that's why I'm hoping you can take over. Not forever! Just . . . for a day or two?"

I blinked. And then blinked again. "But . . . But . . ."

"Why do you look so surprised? We talked about it this morning, didn't we?"

"I know, but I thought . . . I thought you would still be here with me. I didn't think you were going to take off for the beach!"

"I never confirmed I was on a beach. I told you I was at an undisclosed location. With Oprah. Or not."

"Tell him to tell Oprah I say hello!" Dadi said.

"You're obviously at a beach! I just saw a seagull fly over your head. And anyway, I don't think you can just leave me completely in charge," I said, my voice rising. "There must be rules about stuff like this. Isn't there an age requirement to be president?"

He coughed. "Well . . . it's true, this has never happened before. But there's never been someone like you before, who so clearly needs to be the one in charge of everything!"

Clearly. I glared at my bracelet. "I don't think the rest of the world will agree . . ."

"Not true! Both sides of the aisle will agree! And I'm positive that I, or maybe you, can sign an executive order or something about this. We'll figure it out. No worries! You got this."

"I *don't* got this!" My voice choked up. "I'm really nervous. The fate of the country can't be in my hands, Mr. President. Please come back!"

He waved his hand. "Don't worry about it! Everything will be fine. And trust me, a rested president is just what the country needs. I'm sure everything will be great in your capable hands. Just, whatever you do, don't—"

His voice faded out.

"Don't what?" I shrieked. Was there a button I wasn't supposed to press? Someone I wasn't supposed to talk to? What was it?

His voice came back. "Don't announce to the world that you're in charge. We don't want anyone trying to hurt you. Jordan will be following you, of course—"

"Who's Jordan?"

"Head of your Secret Service detail."

"Where is he now?"

"Right behind you."

I turned around and jumped. There was a large man in a black suit and tie standing against the wall. How had I not noticed him?

"Hi," I said.

He nodded.

“Did you know he was there?” I whispered to Dadi.

“Of course I did,” she whispered back, straightening her shoulders. “He’s very handsome.”

“Jordan will protect you,” Mr. President said. “So you’re not really in danger. But we also don’t want everyone in elementary school trying to be president. That would be a disaster. But you, Maya, you’re one of a kind. Thanks again! Did you try a cookie? You should have a cookie!”

And then he took a sip of a tall pink drink that had a tiny umbrella sticking into a slice of pineapple, gave me a salute, and ended the call.

* 11 *

Kid in Chief

I turned to Dadi and didn't know whether to laugh or cry. Or both.

Instead, I got angry.

"How in the world . . . What is he . . . When did I . . . no training . . . What?" I sputtered, waving my arms around.

Dadi came over and put her hands on my shoulders.

"Maya," she said firmly. "Think of all the amazing things people in your family have done for generations."

"What?" I was too busy trying not to hyperventilate to think about anything else.

"Like your grandfather, may Allah grant him peace. Look at all he did to make America a better, healthier place after moving here as a student, working as a scientist to fight infectious diseases. Imagine how proud he would be right now."

"I know, but—"

"If only I could call Farida," Dadi sighed. "But listen, I'm telling you, you can do this. And besides, I'm right here with you."

Alessandra walked into the room holding a stack of binders and a fancy pen in a box. She put them on the desk, motioned me over, and pointed.

"Congratulations on your assignment. Sign here, please," she said.

"Like, my own name?"

"Yes, please. On the line."

I figured I should probably skip the little heart at the end. It didn't seem right for this moment.

My name was typed in bold print at the bottom of the page. *Maya Amir. Acting Commander in Chief.* If I didn't feel the bracelet warm on my wrist, I would be convinced that I was dreaming. But instead, I lifted the heavy, fancy blue pen, signed my name, and, before I could stop myself, added the heart.

Alessandra gave me a side-eye when she noticed the heart but didn't say anything.

There was a knock on the door, and a line of people in suits filed in.

"These are the appointments you've got on your schedule for the morning. I'll introduce you and then you can get started," Alessandra said.

"Okay." I stood up extra tall, brushed the cookie crumbs off my suit, and tried to look as commanding as possible.

"This is Mildred Wilson, Department of the Interior; Maryam Fieldstone, Association of Semiconductor Engineers; Chris Jeffries, National Endowment for the Arts; Lamine Thiam, ambassador of Senegal; and of course, you probably recognize Greg Sussford, vice president."

I gulped as I shook everyone's hands before they settled onto the couches.

Dadi grimaced a little behind the vice president's back, and I remembered her frowning at the TV whenever his name came up. I made a mental note to ask her about him later.

I sat in the big chair behind the desk and as people began to talk, I tried to pretend that I understood what was happening.

"We need emergency funds for six bridges that need repairs!" said one of the women, whose name I'd already forgotten, thrusting a map in my face. "Can you authorize a release?"

"The semiconductor shortage is going to affect prices of electronic exports," another woman explained. "We are going to need an intervention ASAP."

"We're looking to expand our task force and would like some recommendations," a man said. "Here are some potential names."

"My country is very grateful for our friendship, but we are in urgent need of more health system financing," the ambassador said. I remembered who he was because of his cool printed shirt and his accent.

"Um . . ." I looked around at everyone and could feel myself sweating in my suit. This was a *lot* more important than picking dinner or paint colors.

Alessandra came up and whispered in my ear.

"We need you to make quick decisions, ah, Madam President. You have more appointments in fifteen minutes."

"But . . . I don't . . . wait . . ." I stammered. Had she really just called me Madam President?

"I can take care of all this for you, if you like," the vice president volunteered.

"Really?" I said as a flood of relief washed over me. Of course! Being in charge means you can choose to let other people be in charge for you if you want! Perfect!

"Just say the word," the vice president said, smoothing his tie and winking at me. His smile was filled with bright white teeth.

I nodded. Then I noticed that Dadi was glowering at him from across the room. The vice president glanced at her, his eyes lingering on her fuzzy slippers.

"This is my grandmother, Dadi," I said.

"Charmed," Vice President Sussford said, although his smile didn't reach his eyes.

"Can I talk to you for a second, Maya?" Dadi said. "In private?"

"Um. Sure," I said.

Alessandra nodded toward the exit and everyone got up and quickly filed out.

"I'll be right outside the door," Alessandra said, and she stepped out, too.

Dadi turned to me and sighed.

"I don't trust that man, Maya," she said. "His past voting

record, his alliances with the wrong people. He's bad news for this country."

"Vice President Sussford?" I squeaked. "The one who just offered to save me?"

"Maya." Dadi shuffled closer to me in her slippers and I made a mental note to ask Alessandra to get her a change of shoes. "I know you're nervous. But YOU are the one in charge. Don't let this man take away your power. You can get the advice you need, talk to the experts, and make your own decisions."

"But, Dadi, I don't know anything about this stuff. Semiconductors! Infrastructure! Finance! It'll be like what happened at school all over again, but a million times worse."

"What do you mean, school? What happened at school?"

I forgot I hadn't told Dadi about the gerbil, the plunger, or the fire alarms.

"Nothing."

"I'm just saying, listen carefully, ask questions, and if you need other people to support you, make sure they are the right ones, okay?" Dadi searched my face as she spoke.

"Okay," I agreed. I thought I understood her.

Dadi opened the door and Alessandra came back in

with a whole new group of people, along with the vice president.

I tried to take Dadi's advice, and take other people's advice, instead of just listening to what the vice president said. Dadi supplied me with snacks and juice, and made sure I got breaks when she saw me getting overwhelmed. And somehow, together, we got through the rest of the afternoon. I just hoped I could still squeeze in time to check out the bowling lanes.

12

Safety First

I closed my bedroom door and sighed. My day was finally, finally over. So many meetings. So many decisions.

Dadi yawned. "I'm taking a hot shower and going straight to bed. You okay, meri jaan?"

I nodded and glanced at the clock on the wall.

It was eleven thirty. Eleven thirty! I had been up for so many hours! How was I even still standing? I kicked off my shoes, stripped off my rumpled suit jacket, and fell face-first onto my perfectly made bed. I was definitely too tired to go bowling, even though I'd been waiting all day for the chance.

What a day.

Had I made the right decisions? I had no idea. How could I have? I am only ten! What a mess. Was the president coming back tomorrow? Or did I have to do this all again?

Outside the window, I saw flashing lights. What was that? Was the president back? *Please be back.*

I didn't have the energy to get off the bed, so instead I just shimmied closer to the window.

I watched multiple guards surrounding someone on the lawn. Who was that? My heart raced. Was someone trying to hurt me? The president had warned me . . .

I saw a flash of blond hair. A beige coat.

Oh no. Oh, wow.

It was Eloise!

I jumped off my bed and ran out the door into the hallway.

"Mr. Jordan!" I asked. "What's happening outside?"

The Secret Service agent was talking softly on a walkie-talkie but looked up at me. "We have it under control, Madam President."

"But . . . what's going on?"

"There was an intruder. But you do not have to worry. The intruder has been arrested."

ARRESTED? Eloise was arrested? "Don't you think that's a little harsh?" I asked. "I think it's someone I know.

Eloise? She's not the best person on the planet but she's not really dangerous . . ."

"She had a blowtorch on her, ma'am."

Uh-oh. Right. "Yeah, but there was a reason for that . . . I think we can release her . . ."

"I'm sorry, but it's security protocol and we need to take the utmost precautions. Citizens can't just barge into the White House uninvited. With blowtorches."

"I get that," I said, nodding.

"Anything else?"

"Do you think you could at least maybe send her some cookies?" I asked, feeling guilty. I *had* asked Eloise to help me get the bracelet off.

"I'll look into it, ma'am. Anything else?"

"Do you know if the president is coming back tomorrow?"

"I'm not sure, Madam President."

"Okay. Thanks."

I retreated into my room. Dadi was still in the shower and I was glad she'd missed the commotion. I took out the iPad and tried calling the president back at the number he'd called me from before.

No answer.

Great. Just great. This was ridiculous. Where was the president? He couldn't just disappear! He had responsibilities!

I called Alessandra next.

"Yes, Madam President?"

"When is the real president back? Can I go back to school tomorrow?"

"School? Tomorrow? Definitely not," she said. "Tomorrow is an incredibly important day."

"Why? What's happening?"

"It's a big HUSH-HUSH global all-day meeting."

"What do you mean HUSH-HUSH?"

"It's top secret!"

"From who?"

"Everyone!"

"About what?"

"It's HUSH-HUSH!"

"I don't care! I want to go home!" I ended the call and closed my eyes.

The bathroom door opened. "What are you yelling about?" Dadi asked me. She was wearing new pajamas with the White House logo on them.

"I don't want to be here," I said. "I want to go home. I'll sleep on the blow-up mattress, I don't care."

"Maya," she said sternly. "You can't quit."

I blinked back tears. "Why not?"

"This is a gift! You have been given an amazing opportunity and responsibility—and you must take it."

"But I don't want it!"

"We don't always want our responsibilities," she said. "But that doesn't mean we can give them away. They're still ours to carry."

"But—"

She shook her head. "No buts. Also, if you leave, the vice president will take over and he is no good! You can't let that happen."

"It's not my job to—"

"It *is* your job. You have to be strong, Maya. Now go wash up for bed."

"Argh." I picked up my iPad, stormed into the bathroom, and slammed the door.

Instead of washing up, I sat on the edge of the bathtub and called the Best Wishes girls.

Lucy answered right away. "Maya! I haven't been able to sleep worrying about you! What's happening there? Are you going to be on the news?"

Then Becca answered, sleepily. "Hello?"

Oops. I remembered how late it was.

Then Addie appeared, her face lit up by the light of the screen. "I'm under my covers," she whispered. "My parents will ground me if I wake up my sister."

"Sorry it's so late!" I said. "I forgot! But everything is bananas here. I run the country now! The president is MIA! I can't go home! My life is a mess!"

"That is bananas," Becca said.

"It's so cool," Lucy said.

"It sounds terrifying!" Addie said.

"It is all of those things," I said. "And Eloise is in jail!"

"WHAT?" they all shrieked.

"She came to find me here at the White House with a blowtorch! The Secret Service got her," I explained.

"No way," said Becca.

Addie gasped.

"Serves her right," said Lucy.

"I tried to send her cookies," I said. "I felt bad. I asked her for help!"

"Do not ask her for help!" Addie said.

"She doesn't deserve cookies!" Lucy added.

"I just want to go home," I said. "Any ideas how to make that happen?"

They all shook their heads.

"No idea," said Addie.

"The bracelet will come off eventually," Becca said.

"Will it?" I snapped. "How do you know? You don't know, do you? Just because you figured out how to get the bracelet off doesn't mean I will. I could mess up the entire world! There are real stakes here! And this is all your fault! All three of you!"

"Our fault?" Lucy asked. "It is not!"

"It is, too!" I said. "You should never have sent me the bracelet! Or you should have warned me!"

"I wrote you an entire book of warning," Lucy said. "Remember? You read it!"

I shook my head. "Well, you should have warned me MORE."

Becca frowned. "I'm sorry, but—"

"I am so mad at you all right now!" I yelled. Then I ended the call. I put the iPad down on the floor. I stomped my foot. I stomped my other foot.

"Maya?" Dadi called from the other room. "Who were you talking to?"

"No one!" I called back. "I'll be right there."

I washed up and tried to calm down. I slowly changed

into the soft, plush White House pajamas folded on the counter for me. They even had the presidential seal on the top pocket.

By the time I went back into the bedroom, Dadi was already under her covers, quietly snoring.

I turned off the overhead light and climbed into my own bed.

Besides the fact that this bed felt like floating on a giant cloud, everything was pretty terrible. I was scared. I was lonely.

Sure, I was in the White House.

But I was trapped in the White House.

13
Reinforcements

Dadi and I had a tense but delicious breakfast in our private dining room. There were fresh bagels in every flavor. Smoked salmon. Cream cheese. Chocolate pastries. Homemade apple butter. Crystal pitchers filled with fresh OJ and pineapple juice. And plenty of tea for Dadi with hot milk and cardamom, just the way she likes it. The staff at the White House were really on top of their game.

The food was nice, but I wished I was home having cereal and getting ready for school instead of waiting for a HUSH-HUSH meeting. I wished I was wearing jeans and a comfy T-shirt and not another stiff suit that looked exactly like the one I wore yesterday, only gray. I wanted to wear a colorful headband, and not this boring bun that Dadi made for me again.

Was the president ever coming back? I had no idea. Would I have to live in the White House until the next election? Or forever? The thought made me lose my appetite and I put down the second chocolate pastry I'd been about to eat.

I also felt bad about how I'd snapped at the Best Wishes girls the night before. I took out my iPad and typed:

Me: Hey. I'm really sorry about what I said last night. I'm freaking out, but I shouldn't have taken it out on you!

Addie: We understand!

Lucy: We all freaked out too!

Becca: We are always here for you, Maya! ❤

My eyes filled up, and I typed back:

Me: Thanks. You are good friends.

And it was true.

I squared my shoulders and stood up. Time to face the music. Dadi and I headed to the conference room.

"So what is this HUSH-HUSH meeting?" I asked Alessandra as we walked.

"It's a climate meeting," she told us. "Global leaders from all over the world will be there."

"Oh!" I perked up. The climate was something I knew about. Not as much as the global leaders, obviously. But still. It was pretty much my favorite topic. Maybe my luck was changing?

Alessandra flung open the double doors to the conference room.

There were about twenty people already seated around a massive wooden table. Luckily, this time, everyone had their names and roles printed on cards sitting on the table in front of them. I gulped hard as I looked around at all the very important people in one room. The prime minister of Canada! The president of Turkmenistan! The prime minister of Australia! The prime minister of Pakistan! The chancellor of Germany! The president of Ecuador! The president of Ghana! And many more.

Alessandra directed me to the head of the table, and I sat down in a gigantic leather chair that felt like it was swallowing me. I sat up as tall as I could. Dadi took the chair next to me.

The vice president was seated on my other side, and I was relieved to see his familiar face, even though I knew Dadi wasn't a fan.

"Good morning. Shall we call this meeting to order?" he asked me.

"Yes, please," I said softly.

Everyone stared at me, waiting.

"Madam President, this is your meeting," the vice president said in a low voice.

"Right. Okay, here goes." I cleared my throat and spoke as loudly as I could. "Hi, everyone, I'm Maya. I mean, President Amir. Madam President. I mean, you can call me Maya. I'm just filling in for today. I think. But I'm glad we're having this HUSH-HUSH meeting about the climate because the environment is very important to me. And I think it should be important to everyone." The words had poured out of me easily, because I meant them.

Everyone around the table nodded and smiled at me. Maybe this wouldn't be so hard?

Alessandra handed me a folder, which had an agenda inside it. She pointed to the top line.

"Okay, so we're going to hear from some experts now," I said.

Over the next hour, we listened to three people talk about carbon emissions, greenhouse gases, rising sea levels, and more. It was fascinating, but it was a lot of information to take in at once. I was glad Alessandra was taking notes.

The president of Ecuador raised his hand, and I motioned for him to speak.

"This information and data are all important, but what about responsibility?" he asked. "Are you saying that the United States of America and other rich nations will finally take the lion's share of blame for the climate crisis?"

"Um." I paused. Had I said that? I hadn't meant to. I looked at the folder in front of me to see if the answer was in there. It wasn't.

"We demand action!" the president of Ghana added, banging his hand on the table. "Are you admitting that you have not done enough to reduce dependence on fossil fuels?"

Um, yeah, I could definitely admit that my one day as president of the school environmental club hadn't made a massive impact on fossil fuels. But as for the country? "I'm not really sure," I mumbled.

"How are we going to reach global greenhouse gas

emission goals without more technology and financial assistance from you?" the prime minister of Malaysia asked. He looked around the room for agreement and the others nodded.

"Respectfully, this is your meeting, Madam President," the president of Mauritania said to me. "What are you going to do to avert this global crisis? Immediately?"

And just like that, the room erupted. Everyone was talking at once. And soon they were yelling. The more they yelled, the scarier it got. I saw people's eyes bulging out of their heads, and veins popping in their necks. There was sweating. And swearing. And I was afraid that someone was going to start crying for their binky.

But this time, that someone was probably going to be me.

"Order!" Vice President Sussford bellowed.

The room quieted down, and everyone turned to look at him.

"This is no way to make progress!" he said disdainfully. "Blaming and shaming will get us nowhere. We must look forward, and work together to have an impact!"

Everyone looked slightly embarrassed, and suddenly I felt a rush of appreciation for Vice President Sussford, no matter what Dadi said.

He continued speaking. "I've been telling the president for years now that it's simply unreasonable to allow innocent people to suffer, just because of the actions of others."

Most everyone in the room murmured their agreement.

"We will just have to find a way to share this planet, in a way that's acceptable to everyone," he concluded, flashing his white teeth.

Then he turned to me and whispered:

"Now just come up with some silly resolutions and let's get this whole charade over with. We can't seriously let some phony-baloney scientists tell us what we can and can't do with our natural resources! How dare they criticize our steak dinners and private jets. And don't get me started on the whole cutting down trees business! Ever hear of toilet paper? Indispensable! We just need to get everyone to calm down and get our friends in the media to give us some good headlines. And then we can get back to what matters: the next election!" The vice president winked at me when he said the last part.

Uh-oh. That wasn't where I thought he was going with this. Phony-baloney scientists? Friends in the media? Toilet paper?

I turned to Dadi with a helpless shrug. But she clicked

her tongue and said something in Urdu so only I and probably the prime minister of Pakistan could understand.

"You're in charge," she said, "and you need to act like it and do something about this. Fast."

And no matter how tired and frustrated and scared I was by this whole situation, I realized she was right.

"Excuse me, everyone," I said. "I think we need a little break. Why don't you all go to the Oval Office for . . . um, some cookies, and we can meet back here in an hour, okay?"

Alessandra opened up the doors, and the room emptied out quickly.

I guess everyone needed a cookie. And speaking of toilet paper, maybe a bathroom break.

"This is a lot, isn't it?" Dadi asked me.

I nodded. "I just . . . I just wish I knew who to trust. I thought Vice President Sussford was being helpful, but . . ."

"Not so much," Dadi said.

"Right." I sighed. "And the other leaders seem very smart, but . . . they all have their own agenda, you know?"

"So who do you trust?" she asked me.

"You. The rest of our family. My friends."

"So . . ." She waited for me to figure it out.

"If only they were here . . ."

She raised an eyebrow. "And why can't they be?"

Oh! I guess they could be. I was the president. Why couldn't I call a meeting of people I trusted? My very own situation room.

I stood up from the table. "Alessandra?"

She jumped to attention. "Yes?"

"Can you call the motorcade?"

We went to my house first to pick up Mama, Baba, Omar, Natasha, Auntie, and Sabrina. Next we picked up Ms. Maxwell, Leo, and of course, Hazel. Sure, she wasn't the best environmental club president, but she's smart, passionate, and has a great head for science. Plus, she's my best friend.

We drove everyone back to the White House. They all had to sign nondisclosure agreements, promising not to tell anyone they were here, but they didn't mind.

I contemplated sending Air Force One to pick up Becca, Addie, and Lucy, but that didn't seem like the most environmentally friendly idea. We FaceTimed them in and they sent their NDAs back via email.

We were ready to start.

This time I stood at the head of the table.

"Thank you for coming," I told my friends and family.

"Um, so this is really cool and all, but *why* exactly are we here?" Hazel asked.

"I need your help," I said. "I have to come up with an environmental action plan. And I need your input."

"Why us?" Leo asked. "You're the one in charge."

"Yes," I said. "But you all have great ideas, work hard at everything you do, and care about other people. And most importantly, I trust you. Even you, Omar."

"Those are all good reasons," Baba said, smiling proudly. Omar smirked at me, but I could tell he was happy to help.

"I learned from Dadi that food waste is a huge contributor to global warming," I began. "At school I was focused on composting—which is super important—but at the restaurant the other day I saw that the problem is having so much food waste in the first place! Today I learned that all this food waste contributes to eight percent of greenhouse gas emissions. We can do better! And something that seems small can make a big difference."

"That makes a lot of sense," Becca said from FaceTime.

"And I thought we could start by brainstorming together. How can we solve this issue? Can someone write down the ideas on the whiteboard?"

My sister jumped out of her chair. "On it!"

"Thanks, Natasha." I looked around and nodded at Alessandra, who was busy taking notes on the whole meeting. That was really helpful. If only she could do that for me in school.

"Who wants to start sharing ideas?" I asked.

No one said anything.

"Okay. I'll start, then," I said. "What if we can set up some rules so restaurants throw away less food? Can anyone add to that?"

My mother raised her hand.

"Yes, Mama?"

"What about grocery stores? Maybe we can get people to buy perishable foods in smaller amounts and eat the foods before they spoil?"

"Yes!" I cheered. "Great idea!"

My sister wrote everything down on the whiteboard.

Then everyone started sharing ideas. Tax incentives for zero food waste. Standardizing expiration dates so people don't throw away usable food. Fixing supply chain issues. Rescuing unused food from farms and restaurants.

I asked follow-up questions when I wasn't sure I understood. I asked Alessandra to call in experts when I wanted to get more information. I made sure to listen to Hazel's ideas about how to raise awareness and get community support for new programs.

"Instead of posters and flyers, which, um, I guess aren't the best choice for the planet," she said, "we can use social media ads. But we'll still make them really sparkly! And add music! And get celebrity endorsements!"

"That all sounds great," I said with a smile.

Ms. Maxwell suggested promoting hydroponic farming for every household and got a big thumbs-up from Dadi.

Omar suggested using a reward program for kids who take their leftover lunches back home, which was really smart.

I considered everything that everyone had to say.

Then I asked if they could please leave me alone to think for a bit. Everyone nodded and filed out one by one. I blocked out all the voices and reviewed Alessandra's notes.

An hour later I invited the world leaders to come back, one at a time, to listen to my plan.

They each gave me some more ideas and notes and I made some tweaks.

Then I asked Alessandra to help me draft the Food Waste Reduction Plan into an executive order.

I gathered my crew as well as all the world leaders back in the room.

Becca, Addie, and Lucy smiled at me from the iPad.

Finally, as president, I took out the heavy presidential pen and signed the executive order with a flourish. Maya Amir! With a little heart at the end.

It looked so good! And it was one small way to get everyone in the country involved in fighting climate change.

Everyone clapped and cheered. Everyone except Vice President Sussford, that is. He scowled and left the room.

"Yay, Maya!" whooped Omar.

Hazel ran over and threw her arms around me. "Great job, Maya! I'm so proud of you."

"Thank you," I told her, so happy she was here and that we could do this together. And as she beamed at me, I knew she felt the same way as I did, magic or not.

"Thanks, to all of you," I said to everyone in the room, meaning it. "I couldn't have done it without you. You all taught me the most important thing about being a good leader—it's not just about being the boss, or making decisions. It's about teamwork. It's about getting good advice, and surrounding yourself with people you trust, even if they think differently from you. Maybe especially if they do. It's about getting things done."

I held the executive order up so everyone could see my signature, and that's when I saw it—

The clasp!

There was a clasp on my bracelet! The clasp had appeared!

"Becca! Addie! Lucy! Look!" I shoved my wrist in front of the iPad.

My friends and family in the conference room looked puzzled.

"You did it!" Lucy cheered.

"I'm so proud of you!" said Becca.

"So it's done?" I asked, hoping.

"Almost," Addie said.

"What do I do now?" I asked, fiddling with the clasp.

"I think you need someone to take it off for you," Lucy said.

"Dadi," I said, turning to my grandma. "Can you do something else for me?"

"Anything, meri jaan," she said.

I put out my hand. "Will you take this bracelet off for me? There's a clasp now."

"Sure. But why?"

I smiled. "So we can go home."

She looked confused but bent her head down and scrunched up her face. "One second . . . Here you go."

The next thing I knew, the bracelet was off and in my hand.

I heaved a sigh of relief.

A new FaceTime call flashed across the iPad. It was the president!

"I'll talk to you later, okay?" I told the Best Wishes girls. They waved and blew kisses.

I accepted the call. "Hi, Mr. President!"

"Maya!" He smiled. "Hi! How'd you do?"

"Pretty well," I said, and I actually believed that was true. "I'm kind of tired, though."

He nodded. "Being in charge is exhausting, isn't it?"

"Totally."

"I bet you could use a vacation."

"I really could!"

"Well, I'll be back in a few hours. So, you're almost off the hook. And then you can go back to your regular life."

"Really?"

"Really."

"Hurrah!" I cheered. "Mr. President?"

"Yes, Maya?"

"Can I take the pen?"

"Which pen?" he asked.

I lifted up the fancy blue one I had just used. "This one!"

"Sure!"

"Thank you! And, oh, just one more thing," I added.

"Yes?"

"Tell Oprah my dadi says hi!"

"Will do! Maybe! If she's here. Which I can't comment on. See you soon, Maya!"

He hung up.

Dadi gave me a hug. "What now?" she asked.

I smiled at my friends and family. "Anyone want to go bowling?"

14

My Own Bed

We got home that evening, and over dinner, I finished filling my family in on everything I was allowed to share with them about my time at the White House. I was putting away dishes in the kitchen when I heard my brother shout from the living room.

"OMG, MAAYYYYYYYAAAAA! You better get over here! They're back!" Omar yelled.

This time, I didn't doubt that he was serious. And sure enough, there were the flashing blue lights, the motorcycles, and the flags of the presidential motorcade outside the window. Again! And there were the nosy neighbors, peeking through their curtains. Again!

What now? I wasn't wearing the bracelet anymore. What could the president possibly want from me?

When the Secret Service agent came up to the front door, this time I flung it open before he knocked.

"Hello, Miss Amir." He nodded with no expression on his face. I guess I wasn't Madam President anymore, and I was okay with that. But couldn't he at least be friendly?

"Hi, Mr. Jordan," I said cheerfully, and then I followed him straight to the car. My family followed behind me. This time, if I was going anywhere, I was taking them ALL with me.

The window rolled down and I saw the president sitting inside. He definitely looked tanner than a couple of days ago.

"Hi, Mr. President. What's up?" I asked.

"Dinner!" the president said. "For you and Dadi and the rest of your family. I'd like to treat you to a nice meal as a special thank-you for all your hard work over the past couple of days. You pick the spot."

"But we already ate—" Omar started to say, before Natasha jabbed him in the ribs. "Ow!"

"Thank you!" I said. "That would be really nice. And I have the perfect place in mind."

We all got into different cars and drove to Founding

Farmers. It was late and they had just closed and were cleaning up, but they happily opened back up again when the motorcade showed up.

Chef Jackie was beside herself when she saw the president walk into the restaurant. We took the table by the window and the president looked at the menu.

"Can you pick for me?" he asked. "What do you recommend?"

"Definitely the chicken and waffles!" I said with a laugh.

"The pot pie is better!" Omar added.

"I like the quinoa bowl," Natasha volunteered.

The president went with my suggestion. Which was for sure the right decision.

While we ate, the president talked about how much he appreciated what I'd done. He said he was grateful for our discretion, which meant that he didn't want us to tell anyone about the HUSH-HUSH meeting or anything else that had happened, since it was classified. And we all promised not to say a word to anyone.

"Does that mean she can't put being president on her college applications?" Dadi asked.

"Unfortunately, no," he said with a laugh. "But I can absolutely put in a good word for you when the time comes."

Wow.

"And," the president went on, "hearing about how well you handled yourself made me realize that I need a new running mate in the next election. Someone who will put the interests of the country first. That will no longer be Vice President Sussford."

"Oh, thank Allah!" Dadi burst out, which made us all grin.

"Can it be Maya?" Omar asked, and everyone laughed while I shook my head.

"But I do hope that you'll consider a future in politics, Maya," the president said to me, his voice serious. "You have a bright future ahead of you, and our nation could benefit from a mind like yours."

I blushed from the praise and was too tongue-tied to answer. But Dadi chimed in, saying that she always knew that I took after my grandfather.

"I actually think I take after you, Dadi," I told her.

She couldn't help but smile.

The president turned to Dadi.

"We'd love to have you back at the White House sometime. Maybe you could help out with a new hydroponic garden? I heard you've got quite the green thumb!"

Dadi dropped her spoon when he said that. But the rest

of us cheered. If anyone belonged at the White House, it was Dadi.

As I looked around the table, I was so grateful for my family, and for every single thing that happened from the minute that bracelet came into my life.

After we finished our second dinner at Founding Farmers, we said good-bye to the president and went home. Then Auntie and Sabrina left to go back to Pittsburgh. "Best DC trip ever," Sabrina said as she and Auntie hugged me.

I texted the Best Wishes girls to thank them for their help, and then started typing a text to Hazel.

I hesitated. I wanted to remain the environmental club president. But Hazel deserved it, too.

Me: Thanks again for your help today!

Hazel: Of course! You were amazing.

Me: I'm wondering . . . would you consider being co-president of the club with me? I could really use your help. You're so good at marketing!

Hazel: That sounds amazing 🥳

Me: 🎉

I smiled and put down my phone. And then, for the first time in what felt like ages, I went to sleep in my regular bed, in my regular room, wearing regular pajamas. And I slept really, really well.

When my eyes popped open the next morning, for a second, I felt a pang of sadness that my wish and adventures were over. But then I remembered last night and smiled again.

Now the house was quiet, and it sounded like everyone was sleeping in this Saturday morning. I got up quietly and decided to make breakfast for my family. After all, I'd run the country! Sort of. So I could totally do this.

I washed some fruit, took out some yogurts, heated up toast, and made tea for Dadi, with plenty of hot milk and cardamom.

When everyone was up, we all sat around the table and ate.

"Thank you for preparing breakfast," Dadi told me. "That was delicious."

"Maybe you could teach me how to make your desi omelet?" I asked her.

She winked. "Definitely!"

"It was great," Mama said. "Thank you."

"Omar and I will clean up," Natasha said.

Hurrah!

I went back to my room and stretched out on my bed. I wished I still had the presidential iPad but took out the old iPhone instead.

I FaceTimed the Best Wishes crew.

"Hi, Madam President!" Becca said.

"How does it feel to be a regular person again?" Addie asked.

"It feels . . . calm," I told her. "It's nice to be home."

"I'm sure!" Becca said.

"I'll miss having my own bowling alley, though."

"Maybe we can get the next person who gets the bracelet to wish for that," Addie said.

"Oh! Right! Maya, tell us who's next!" Lucy said.

"What do you mean?" I asked.

"Whose name does it say on the red package?" Addie asked. "Where are you sending the bracelet?"

OMG. Of course! In all the excitement, I hadn't even checked. "Let me call you right back!"

I hung up and ran to the laundry room, where I had left the box. I had hidden it under the sink.

I reached down and pulled out the box.

I ran back to my room with the box and immediately called the girls.

"It's going to someone named Emma!" I told them.

"Oooh!" Addie cheered. "I love the name Emma."

"I wonder what she's like," Becca said.

"Maybe we can all meet one day," Lucy said. "In person!"

"How fun would that be!" I said.

"It really would," Becca said. "You should all come to New York!"

"Or you're welcome in DC anytime," I told the girls.

"Do you think the president would let us use his jet?" Addie said.

"Speaking of people who have their own jets . . ." Becca said ominously. "Where is Eloise?"

I almost dropped the iPhone. Eloise! Oh no! "I forgot about Eloise!"

Lucy gasped. "No you didn't!"

I started laughing. "I totally did. She's still in jail!"

"Maya, you have to get her out," Lucy said.

"Do you?" Becca asked.

"Yes!" Addie agreed. "I think?"

"You do," Becca said. "But maybe not this very second.

Maybe wait until you mail off the package. So she can't follow it."

"And then maybe give it another week or two," Lucy said.

We all laughed.

"You know what you have to do now, don't you?" Addie asked me.

"Take a nap?" I asked, stretching out on my bed. "This week was exhausting."

"Yes," Becca said. "But also write down what happened to you! So you can send Emma a letter. To put in her package. Like Lucy did for you."

"And Addie did for me," Lucy said.

"And Becca did for me," Addie said.

"You're right," I said. "Having you all to talk through everything was the best part of getting the bracelet."

"Aw," said Lucy. "Thanks."

"I hope we didn't stress you out," Addie said.

"You did a little," I said. "But it was totally worth it. Becca, I don't know how you managed the magic bracelet without a crew."

"Seriously," Addie said. "Thank you for starting the chain, and writing me your story."

Becca smiled. "Happy to. And now it's up to Maya to keep the chain going!"

"On it," I told them. "I'll start right now. I'll text you all later, 'kay?"

"'Kay!" they all said.

And then I was off.

First, I found an extra notebook in the kitchen.

Then I sat at my desk and started writing to you.

So.

Hi, Emma!

Thank you for reading my whole story.

I know it sounds impossible. Bananas. Out of this world.

But it's all true.

And now that you've finished reading, please call or text me! My contact info—and Becca's, Addie's, and Lucy's—is on the inside of this book. It's a small, magical, sparkly world, and it's our job to take care of it—and one another. We can't wait to meet you.

Best wishes,

maya♡

READ ALL ABOUT BECCA'S, ADDIE'S, AND LUCY'S ADVENTURES IN:

Acknowledgments

Thank you to all the wonderful people who helped us with this book.

Jen Bricking, who created the gorgeous art and the beautiful cover.

Aimee Friedman, our amazing editor, for working her magic on this story.

Laura Dail and Matthew Elblonk, our brilliant agents.

Thank you to everyone at Scholastic, especially Elizabeth B. Parisi, Cianna Sanford, Melissa Schirmer, David Levithan, Abby McAden, Ellie Berger, Rachel Feld, Katie Dutton, Erin Berger, Seale Ballenger, Lia Ferrone, Brooke Shearouse, Lizette Serrano, Emily Heddleson, Elizabeth Whiting, and everyone in Sales and in the School Channels.

Thanks to Austin Denesuk, Matthew Snyder, and Berni

Barta at CAA. Everyone at Lion Forge Entertainment and Eydie Faye.

Thanks to the fabulous Lauren Walters, Nicole Caliro, and all our writer friends!

Special thanks to Debbie Rigaud and Christina Soontornvat, our Best Wishes crew.

Thank you to all our family: Farrukh, Bilal, and Humza, and Todd, Chloe, and Anabelle.

About the Authors

SARAH MLYNOWSKI is the *New York Times* and *USA Today* bestselling author and coauthor of over fifty books for tweens, teens, kids, and adults, including the Whatever After series, the Best Wishes series, and the Upside-Down Magic series, which was adapted into a Disney Channel movie. Originally from Montreal, Sarah now lives in Los Angeles with her family. Visit her online at sarahm.com and find her on social media @sarahmlynowski.

HENA KHAN has been publishing books for children, including many that center Pakistani American and Muslim characters, for over two decades. She writes picture books, middle grade fiction, pick-your-path adventures, and graphic novels. Her book *Amina's Voice* was named best book of the year by the *Washington Post*, NPR, and *Kirkus*. Its sequel, *Amina's Song*, won the Asian/Pacific American Award for Children's Literature. Hena was born and raised outside Washington, DC, where she still lives with her family. Visit her online at henakhan.com.